Praise for
BROKEN HEARTS MENDED

Healing from Divorce

"This is a masterfully written book that everyone should read, both those who are going through difficult trials as well as those who are not, so that they can be more understanding and helpful to those who are. Once started, it is difficult to put down. It is based on sound wisdom and sound gospel principles. The writing style is immediately captivating and keeps the interest level high throughout."

—David J. Ridges, best-selling author of the Gospel Studies Made Easier series and *100 Signs of the Times*

"Reg's book is a wonderful study on how one can deal with and successfully move ahead in life and in the gospel after suffering the devastating experience of divorce. His counsel is the same counsel everyone needs in overcoming that or any other trial we face in life. He teaches us how to live the gospel to the fullest, be forgiving, keep our covenants, love with all our hearts, and to always look forward with faith rather than backward with bitterness and regret. I recommend this tremendously spiritual book to any and all who need to be lifted from despair and heartache of any kind."

—Clair M. Poulson, Latter-day Saint author and justice court judge

"*Broken Hearts Mended: Healing from Divorce* will bring hope to one of life's most difficult challenges. Reg Christensen's personal experience, his spirituality and keen writing ability will bring peace and understanding to the troubled soul. I highly recommend this work to anyone who needs direction as they come to understand and navigate the trials and heartache of divorce."

—Ed Cox, general manager and president of CentraCom and a former Sanpete County commissioner

"The heartache of divorce touches nearly everyone in some way. There are few books that give concrete steps to finding healing and comfort in the Savior and His gospel following divorce. This one does. Brother Christensen writes from experience—sensitively guiding the reader through pain, sadness, and loss to the peace and joy Christ offers. I highly recommend it!"

—Rosemary R. Lind, wife, mother, grandmother, and former teacher and editor

"Despite making vows and covenants, the love story ends, and marriages are terminated in divorce. The resulting shock, pain, uncertainty, and fear of the future leave families with hands hanging down and knees that are weak. Reg does a marvelous job of leading the reader through God-given and time-tested steps to not only survive divorce but to find the joy and happiness that we previously envisioned when we shouted for joy at the opportunity to come here! There can be wonderfully bright days ahead! Days filled with marvelous relationships, stability and peace of mind for all who will trust in the Lord with all their hearts and let him direct their paths! You will want to read and reread this handbook for dealing with divorce."

—Tom Boyer, national and international agricultural leader and consultant

BROKEN HEARTS MENDED

Healing from Divorce

Reg Christensen

CFI
An imprint of Cedar Fort, Inc.
Springville, Utah

© 2018 Reg Christensen
All rights reserved.

No part of this book may be reproduced in any form whatsoever, whether by graphic, visual, electronic, film, microfilm, tape recording, or any other means, without prior written permission of the publisher, except in the case of brief passages embodied in critical reviews and articles.

This is not an official publication of The Church of Jesus Christ of Latter-day Saints. The opinions and views expressed herein belong solely to the author and do not necessarily represent the opinions or views of Cedar Fort, Inc. Permission for the use of sources, graphics, and photos is also solely the responsibility of the author.

ISBN 13: 978-1-4621-4595-9

Published by CFI, an imprint of Cedar Fort, Inc.
2373 W. 700 S., Springville, UT 84663
Distributed by Cedar Fort, Inc., www.cedarfort.com

LIBRARY OF CONGRESS CATALOGING-IN-PUBLICATION DATA

The Library of Congress has cataloged the previous edition, Losing Everything in Divorce: Finding Healing through Christ, as follows:

Names: Christensen, Reg, author.
Title: Losing Everything in Divorce: Finding Healing through Christ / Reg Christensen.
Description: Springville, Utah : CFI,An imprint of Cedar Fort,Inc., [2018] | Includes bibliographical references and index.
Identifiers: LCCN 2018006060 (print) | LCCN 2018012042 (ebook) | ISBN 9781462122141 (epub, pdf, mobi) | ISBN 9781462122141 (perfect bound : alk. paper)
Subjects: LCSH: Divorce--Religious aspects--Church of Jesus Christ of Latter-day Saints. | Divorce--Religious aspects--Mormon Church.
Classification: LCC BX8643.D58 (ebook) | LCC BX8643.D58 C47 2018 (print) | DDC 248.8/46--dc23
LC record available at https://lccn.loc.gov/2018006060

Cover design by Jeff Harvey
Cover design © 2018 Cedar Fort, Inc.
Edited by Deborah Spencer and Michelle Stoll
Typeset by Kaitlin Barwick

Printed in the United States of America

10 9 8 7 6 5 4 3 2 1

Printed on acid-free paper

Contents

Preface: Broken Hearts Mended vii
   One: All These Things Shall Give Thee Experience 1
   Two: Always Keep Your Eternal Perspective 6
   Three: Honoring Agency 10
   Four: Forgive All 15
   Five: Eternal Sociality 21
   Six: Keep in Remembrance 26
   Seven: Live in Thanksgiving 33
   Eight: Ye Ought to Search the Scriptures 39
   Nine: Stand Blameless before God 46
   Ten: Correct Doctrine 53
   Eleven: Anxiously Engaged in a Good Cause 63
   Twelve: Unto My Holy Mountain 72
   Thirteen: More Intelligent than They All 78
   Fourteen: Hope for the Children 86
   Fifteen: Always Retain a Remission of Your Sins 94
   Sixteen: True Enduring 101
   Seventeen: Trust in the Lord, and in Thyself 108
Epilogue: The Piercing Light of the Savior's Atonement 114
Acknowledgments 116
About the Author 117

Also by
Reg Christensen

Fear Not: *Messages of Hope, Healing, and Peace in the Book of Revelation* (2010)

Worthy is the Lamb: *Scriptural Insights of Peace and Joy from Handel's Messiah* (2012)

Joyful Apocalypse: *Unveiling the Messages of Joy and Hope in the Book of Revelation* (2013)

Unlocking Isaiah: *Lessons and Insights that Draw Us to the Savior* (2013)

Regular: *The Saga of a Regular Guy from an Extraordinary Place* (2014)

Essays from the Garden: Living Water for your Soul (2022)

Preface

Broken Hearts Mended

"I'm just livin' the dream" was the timeworn cliché I recently heard a young store employee say to a customer. I hope he is living his worthy dreams.

A few decades ago, I felt I really was living my dream. I had a blessed childhood, followed by military and missionary service and college education. Midway through my college days, I met a young lady of strong pioneer heritage. We fell in love, married in the temple, and moved to a new place to complete a college degree. Before graduation, our first son was born. We then moved again to begin my desired profession of teaching released-time seminary. We soon purchased a small home on a large lot in a great neighborhood and, with the arrival of three more children, invested our sweat equity by doing almost all of the work ourselves in more than doubling our home size. As I sawed every board and hammered every nail, I did so with the sweet faith that our home would continue to be a refuge for our family from the storms and trials of life.

While teaching full-time, I completed my master's degree and my wife was able to return to school to complete her degree. We gardened, camped, traveled, played in the winter and summer forests, and much enjoyed our family and friends. We struggled to pay our bills but were blessed with all we needed. We worked hard together as a family in operation of a part-time business to supplement our family economy and to teach our children how to work. We served in the Church as we were called to several organizations. Eventually, I was ordained as bishop of my ward and delighted to have our own teenage children as part of our many youth outings and programs. I truly felt I was living my destiny as I served my family, taught the gospel to the youth of our community, and ministered to our ward members. I share this statement from my personal journal at that time:

> I will conclude the year with this summary statement: My feeling at this time was that I was right in the midst of my destiny. I had a wonderful family . . . and I felt desperately needed by them. I felt much love for [my wife] and was so grateful for our love and relationship. I was square in the trenches of war with Satan through my work as bishop and as seminary teacher. I felt needed, successful, and positive about life. I often had the distinct feeling that the next four or five years of completing my service as bishop and rearing our teenagers to maturity would certainly be the most crucial and important period of my life. My only desire was to be true to my covenants and to succeed in my responsibilities.[1]

And then: "IT IS HEREBY ORDERED, ADJUDGED, AND DECREED THAT the bonds of matrimony heretofore existing by and between the Petitioner and Respondent are hereby dissolved."[2] Our twenty-four-year marriage was over. I was heartbroken—gone from my children and my home, released from my call as bishop, and dismissed from my profession. In my hour of darkness, it seemed that my life had been wasted—everything that I had desired and worked for was gone.[3]

Yes, there is a huge, gaping void here. I will omit the detail of what happened and leave it unexplained since the purpose of this book is to discuss *healing* from divorce, not to share the specifics of how we got to the point of needing to be healed. And although my story may contain many similarities to yours, I am sure there are also many differences. My desire is to share what I consider to be universal principles that will bless all of our lives, no matter what our story or circumstance may be.

Since I have already risked the use of one timeworn cliché, I will venture another—*I feel your pain*. And in this matter of suffering from divorce, for me at least, this is not a mere cliché—it is reality. I am not exaggerating as I speak of seemingly endless nights of sobbing and despair—sometimes wishing the morning would come quickly and other times wishing it would not come at all. Sometimes I wished I could just die. I wrestled for seemingly endless hours with the repetitive questions that rolled like waves through my soul—How will I survive?

What will I do? How will my children survive? Why me? What could and should I have done differently? What are people saying and thinking? Does anyone really know the truth of the matter? Where did I go wrong? Why am I so embarrassed at my status? How dare I go out in public? Why am I avoiding people who have been my truest friends? Will I ever be happily married again? Why do so many familiar experiences and associations now just bring sadness to my heart? Will I ever have an eternal family? Would death of a spouse be an easier trial? Am I losing my mind? Why do some people seem to have such easy lives? What am I supposed to learn from this darkness? Will I ever feel peace? Will my heart ever stop aching? And so on, and so on and so on . . . hour after hour, day after day, week after week, and month after month.[4]

My friend, who had completed his doctoral study on marriage and divorce, informed me that "studies show that it takes seven years to heal from divorce." At first, I did not think I would ever heal. Now that I am a few decades down the road, I wish I could have been fully healed after only seven years. I have now concluded that for me and I suppose for most, *complete* healing will not come in this life, but will, in part, be delayed until "God shall wipe away all tears from their eyes; and there shall be no more death, neither sorrow, nor crying, neither shall there be any more pain: for the former things are passed away" (Revelation 21:4).

However, I am happy to report that much of my broken heart has mended. Now in retrospect I see with increased gratitude the way my Heavenly Father and my Savior held onto me through my darkest days and continue to hold and guide me now as I continue my journey. As I think back to those most difficult and dark months and years at the beginning of my trial and consider with gratitude my blessings from the very outset, I realize now that I *did not* lose everything. My children were and are sealed to me forever. The light of my testimony never faltered. My temple recommend never expired. My eternal hope—although seemingly dim at times—has shone forward as a comforting, guiding, and motivating truth through the years.

If by this writing I can help to encourage you and bless your life by my sharing of true principles, then my goal will be accomplished and my reward will be complete. I hope for nothing more than for those of us who pass through this most challenging trial to hang onto our faith, keep our eternal perspective, and work toward the greatest of all gifts, even eternal life (see D&C 14:7). I sincerely hope that our broken hearts will finally be mended. I believe that they will be.

Notes

1. This statement comes from my personal history, Volume II, Page 6, written at the end of 1995.
2. This citation is from my personal Decree of Divorce from the Fourth Judicial District Court for Utah County, State of Utah.
3. I always knew that the policy of the Church Educational System was that someone divorced could not be employed to teach full time—I just never thought it would apply to me. Also, once we were well into the depth of our struggles, I could no longer function effectively as bishop. The decision for my release came as a mutual agreement between me and my stake president.
4. Even though my marriage was over, I continued, as I had always done, to believe in the principle of marriage, and I actively sought a new companion and married; I will share more details in a later chapter.

One

All These Things Shall Give Thee Experience

Divorce is one of the more severe trials of mortality. I have a few purposes in making such a statement but will first offer a qualifier.

Because we have unique personalities, circumstances, and capacities for learning the lessons of mortality and for bearing trial and pain, we really cannot compare *ourselves* one to another. Our journey through our mortal probation is a highly customized and personalized excursion.

Now having stated that, I repeat that, in my opinion, compared to other *trials*, divorce is one of the more severe trials of mortality. I say this to hopefully elicit a greater degree of empathy from family and friends toward those experiencing divorce. Please be loving and patient for the short and the long terms. I also make my declaration as a sort of preparatory "heads up" to those who may be new to this trial—prepare yourself for the long haul. I have often referred to divorce as "the gift that just keeps on giving."

Although I feel that my own heart is well on the way to being mended, I have also concluded that many heartaches will continue with us until an eternal day beyond our mortal lifetime. For example, the joy you feel for a couple celebrating their golden wedding with all of their happy and well-adjusted children worshipping together in the temple just may also serve as a bitter contrasting reminder of the sadness you may feel at the thought of your own fractured family. You may as well get used to it—it is part of the journey.

I know a young mother of three children who lost her husband to a terrible accident when their youngest daughter was just four months old. She rose above the ashes of despair and married a man who was divorced and had one child. As they are working to blend themselves into a new family, they are experiencing the bitterness of divorce and child custody issues. On multiple occasions, she has lamented to me that the sorrow and challenge of their current trials seem far more severe than her trial at the death of her husband.

I know a woman whose husband abandoned his gospel covenants and left her and their children. Of the dark trial of her divorce, she has remarked, "Once your eternal companion betrays your marriage covenants, all else pales in comparison."

Indeed, you may feel your life is crashing down around you. On the afternoon of January 15, 2009, Captain Chesley "Sully" Sullenberger was in command at takeoff of an Airbus A320 loaded with 155 passengers and crew. After both engines were destroyed by colliding with a flock of Canadian geese, he quickly assessed the loss of power and made preparations for an emergency landing in the Hudson River just off Manhattan. He later described that moment as "the worst, sickening, pit-of-your-stomach, falling-through-the-floor feeling"[1] that he had ever experienced. As he guided the plane into the river channel, Captain Sullenberger gave the command of "brace for impact" which served not only as instruction for the passengers to hang on, but also as code for the crew to execute emergency procedures.

I am confident we can relate to Captain Sullenberger's pit-of-your-stomach feeling. For those of us divorced or divorcing, we need to prepare ourselves for landing as we plunge into the darkness and uncertainty of our new life.

So brace yourself. You may not receive comforting words from the people you would hope to receive them from. You may be harshly judged—or at least it may feel that way. There will not be a powerful, complimentary eulogy offered you for the loss of your spouse. Your children will likely struggle in ways new to them and to you—just love them. Don't expect a lot of flowers. You will not hear the promise that "your family will be together forever because you are sealed in the temple." You will likely continue to hear the plea—and rightly so—to "remember the widow" in act and deed, but don't get your hopes up about the same consideration for those who are divorced. Don't expect a Christmas basket. People may shun you—probably because they just do not know what to say or do. You may receive expressed or implied counsel that had you done better, this would not be happening to you. You may expect to read articles and hear talks about divorce, but prepare yourself that the message may well be "Don't do it" rather than how to heal from it.

Fortunately all of those under the care of Captain Sullenberger and his crew lived—and so will we. Our path to rescue may not be clear at present, but it will happen. So brace yourself. It will be hard and it will be scary. But your broken heart will heal in time. Hang on and hope on and pray always.

I have learned a great deal about meeting the trial of divorce with faith and courage from Emily Hill Woodmansee, who was born in England in March of 1836. She was the youngest of eleven children and enjoyed the favor and privilege of her good parents—until she received a testimony of the restored gospel. At the age of twelve, she was allowed to accompany her cousin six miles away to the adjoining village of Chalford to hear the preaching of the Mormon elders. Emily received a witness of the spirit that the gospel message was true and, upon returning home from the meeting, she informed her family that she intended to join the Mormons as soon as she was old enough. From that day forth, her parents allowed her no more association with the Mormons and she was left to pursue her newfound faith mostly in private. Finally, in March of 1852, at the age of sixteen, Emily was baptized, along with her sister, Julia.

The girls longed to immigrate to Zion and pursued this goal for the next four years, finally receiving the opportunity to sail on the ship *Thornton* in May of 1856. They left England with mixed feelings of joy and excitement at the prospect of gathering with the saints but with continued sadness and a bitter parting from family and friends who had consistently continued to reject their new faith. The girls traveled under the leadership of Elder James Willie. Upon arrival in America, they found their way to Iowa City and were assigned to travel with the famous ill-fated handcart company led by Captain Willie.

Emily and Julia were party to the full spectrum of hardship and suffering experienced by the Willie handcart company. Fatigue, illness, cold, and hunger were their traveling companions. Sorrow and longings for family along with the peace, joy, and hope of the gospel were undoubtedly their emotional partners on this heroic trek. We can only imagine the relief and gratitude they felt at the arrival of the rescuing parties. Although they still had a long journey ahead, and many hardships yet to endure, they were on their way to Zion.

After a brief time in the Salt Lake Valley, Emily and Julia each married men who had been part of their rescue party. Julia's marriage was successful and happy. Emily, however, had more dark clouds on her horizon. After the birth of her first child, her husband went to England on a mission. It was all she could do in his absence to provide for herself and her child as they existed on the constant brink of starvation. And then, four years after her husband had departed, he sent word to her that he was not intending to return. He had abandoned his faith and his marriage covenant. He had betrayed her. Emily shared the following:

> After I had worked upwards of four years to maintain myself and little one, my husband himself sent me word that he never intended to set foot in Utah again. And here I must be allowed to say in behalf of myself and other true women who have endured such separations, and to whom, perhaps, it is counted as nothing, no one can realize what such an ordeal is, unless they have passed through it. *All that I had hitherto suffered seemed like child's play compared to being deserted by the one in whom I had placed the utmost confidence,* who himself had fixed an impassable gulf between us by ignoring the very principles by which he had obtained me, leaving myself and little one (for all he knew) to sorrow and destitution. (emphasis added)[2]

Although I cannot relate to the physical sufferings experienced by Emily, I well know the emotional trauma. My friend and bishop, who replaced me as bishop at the time of my release, counseled me that I would someday be grateful for my trials because I would learn so much from them. I was skeptical of his words then but have since realized the prophetic truth he shared with me. And although I do not say or feel that I am grateful that I got divorced, I can say that I have learned by my own experience the truth of his message. I have learned much and gained great empathy for all who suffer divorce. And I feel that the Lord, in His own way, has often orchestrated my healing from divorce and knowledge gained through this trial to the encouragement and blessing of others. I just know in my heart that the path to eternal life is true and that full and complete healing eventually comes to those who seek it.

I also know that, even though I doubt few, if any of us, would choose divorce as a mortal trial, we are also entitled to the promise of the Lord to His suffering prophet Joseph in Liberty Jail: "all these things shall give thee experience, and shall be for thy good" (D&C 122:7). I believe that, if we are faithful to gospel covenants and commandments, our opportunity for growth and development will be commensurate to the depth of our trial.

Notes

1. Chesley "Sully" Sullenberger, interview by Katie Couric, *60 Minutes,* CBS, Feb. 8, 2009.
2. Edith Ivins Lamoreaux, "Sweet Singers of Zion: Life Sketches of Emily Hill Woodmansee and Julia Hill Ivins," *Relief Society Magazine* 8, no. 10 (1921): 565.

Two

Always Keep Your Eternal Perspective

A few weeks prior to our current service assignment in the Holy Land, I contacted a friend of mine and scheduled a breakfast meeting to see how he was doing and to say goodbye. He is a very intelligent man, holding degrees in theology and formerly serving as the pastor of a large congregation in our area. Our friendship began when a mutual friend introduced us. I then accompanied our missionaries for over a year as we taught him. He continues to pursue a serious-minded analysis of our doctrines. At our goodbye meeting, he informed me that he had been contemplating the economic principle of *added value* and seeking to draw a parallel to the possible benefit or added value he could gain from baptism into our Church. He announced that he had drawn a conclusion. I excitedly asked, "And what have you concluded?" His profound but simple answer was, "eternal life."

The Lord said, "And, if you keep my commandments and endure to the end you shall have eternal life, which gift is the greatest of all the gifts of God" (D&C 14:7). One of my favorite descriptors of eternal life is given by the Lord as He offers a statement of blessing to those who accept and live His gospel: that they go "to their exaltation and glory in all things, as hath been sealed upon their heads, which glory shall be a fulness and a continuation of the seeds forever and ever" (D&C 132:19). "Seeds" refers to posterity—our eternal family.

"But my eternal family has been fractured" may be our lament as we divorce. A friend and former teacher of mine sensed that I may have been feeling that way. When he heard of my divorce, he took time to write me a meaningful and encouraging letter in which he said, "I want to share with you something I heard a member of the Quorum of the Twelve share recently with someone going through a similar struggle— 'Always keep your eternal perspective.'"[1]

As with so many trials and heartaches, if we apply an eternal perspective to them, they become much different than they may seem as we are experiencing them. Yes, the dissolution of your marriage may be final—you and your former spouse may not be together forever in eternity. But with an eternal perspective, we come to remember and better understand that, in due time (whether short or long), eternal life may include a true eternal companion. And we also remember that we are sealed (and if not yet, we may be) to our innumerable ancestors. And we remember that we are sealed (and if not yet, we may be) to our vast line of descendants. And we may remember and understand the capstone sealing of all—that we are sealed (and if not yet, we may be) to our loving Heavenly Mother and Father and unto life eternal, the type of life that They enjoy.

I believe that each child of God has a natural, innate connection to Heavenly Father and a longing for eternal life—life forever with our Heavenly Parents and with our beloved friends and family. As I am writing these words, I have within my view the old city of Jerusalem and the revered sites of the major religions of Judaism, Islam, and Christianity. In our assignments here, we interact daily and personally with members of all of these faiths. Like my mother before me, I am a natural "people watcher." I love observing culture, human nature, and personal interaction. I am humbled and grateful for the many expressions of faith that I see—whether it be the elderly woman crawling on her knees to the stone in the Church of the Holy Sepulcher, kissing it through her tears because she believes Christ's body was prepared for nearby burial there; or the devout Jew reverently placing his written prayer in the stones of the Western Wall; or the Muslim man humbly responding to the call to prayer by rolling out his prayer mat and prostrating himself before God. My sense is that most of these humble people only desire lasting peace and eternal friendship with all of God's children. (And, granted, there are some seen on the evening news who pervert their meager understanding of religion to cause harm one to another, but most of the people I see here live in peace and mutual respect).

My heart has been warmed as I have been privileged to see the personal interactions of our employees here at the BYU Jerusalem Center. For example, my soul smiles each time I see the parting embrace and traditional kiss on the cheeks of our two administrative assistant young ladies in the front office—one Jewish and one Palestinian. And I think I have enough experience in people-watching to know that their expressions are heartfelt—they really do love and care for each other. I believe that we as mortals generally innately care for each other and that the better acquainted we become, the greater is our desire for eternal friendship. I believe that most people have a natural, eternal bond to all of their brothers and sisters in the family of God.

I have also been intrigued by those who come to the Holy Land hoping to exactly pinpoint the historic and sacred sites. People ask me, "Was Christ crucified and buried at the site of the Church of the Holy Sepulcher or at the Garden Tomb site outside the city walls?" I smile and motion toward the more general panorama of Jerusalem and reply, "It happened right here—in Jerusalem."

Let us view our own personal trials in this broad, more eternal way. As we find ourselves deep in the hot flames of the great chasm of despair, feeling that we have failed because our marriage to the one we loved and trusted has ended, we need to "stand still, and see the salvation of the Lord" (Exodus 14:13) and seek understanding of His eternal perspective. Yes, our former spouse may be gone from us, but we have our families, our friends, our broader human family, and our God and our Savior always with us in eternal bonds. And we have a hope of complete healing of our broken hearts and a prospect of eternal life with multitudes of the righteous forever after. Because of the Atonement of Jesus Christ (that happened right here in Jerusalem), we may be rescued from our pain and suffering with assurance that the terrifying gulf between our mortal misery and our eternal felicity is bridged.

Elder Bruce C. Hafen taught, "Sometimes we say that no other success can compensate for our failures in the home. And while it is true that no other success of ours can fully compensate, there is a success that compensates for all our failures, after all we can do in good faith (see 2 Nephi 25:23). That success is the Atonement of Jesus Christ. By its power, we may arise from the ashes of life filled with incomprehensible beauty and joy."[2]

Although our hearts may seem, at present, to be breaking completely apart, let us hold on in faith and always keep our eternal perspective. Our God who knows all knows us—and He will never forget nor betray nor disappoint.

Notes

1. I still have this letter in my file and in my personal history. In respect of the privacy of my friend, I will keep his name anonymous.
2. Bruce C. Hafen, *The Broken Heart: Applying the Atonement to Life's Experiences* (Salt Lake City: Deseret Book, 2008), 26.

Three

Honoring Agency

Just as eternal life, or the type of life enjoyed by our Heavenly Father, is the greatest gift of eternity, the gift and exercise of agency is one of the greatest gifts of mortality. These two gifts are inseparably connected to our mortal and our immortal lives.

Thoughts of eternal life can and should inspire us but may also discourage us, since, as with mere mortal perspective, it may all seem so distant. And it may at times seem so unattainable, particularly as we struggle to keep our heads above the flooding waters of despair as we deal with the sorrows of divorce. God's gift of agency, when properly understood and applied, is a life preserver to lift us from our despair and guide us safely forward.

Often in my teaching years, when a student would suggest that an individual could lose his or her agency through poor choices, I have thrown out a challenge for discussion: "Is there anything you could do to deprive me of or to restrict my agency to choose to follow Christ?" Answers have included beating, defaming, imprisonment, deceiving, kidnapping, and even murder. I have not yet received a convincing response. Any or all of those things could restrict my *freedom to act* as I so desire, but not my *ability to choose* what I believe and who I follow. Even in death, it is our gift to continue to follow our Savior and His gospel.

The prophet Lehi taught, "Wherefore, men are free according to the flesh; and all things are given them which are expedient unto man. And they are free to choose liberty and eternal life, through the great Mediator of all men, or to choose captivity and death, according to the captivity and power of the devil" (2 Nephi 2:27). Our God-given agency is precious and eternal. It cannot be taken from us. We may not take it from others. "We cannot pray away another's agency."[1]

Three: *Honoring Agency*

A few decades ago, my former wife and I, along with two of our children, went on a four-day river trip down the Colorado River. Most of the river is calm and easy, and life jackets are not even worn except in the whitewater. The most treacherous of the whitewater consists of three sets of rapids, appropriately named Big Drop I, II, and III. At this point, the river constricts into the narrow Cataract Canyon as it dramatically drops in elevation. The water rushing down this channel provides one of the most exhilarating whitewater adventures on planet earth.

We did just fine on Big Drop I. However, on the very first wave of Big Drop II, our boat was pushed straight up in the air and back down again—upside down—throwing us out of the boat in all directions.[2] I was thrown far from the boat, so I began to work my way back to it. I did not see my wife, though I later learned that she had surfaced underneath the overturned boat and had then struggled to find an air pocket. As I finally reached the boat, a feeling of terror hit me as I discovered my ankle was caught in its rope. As I frantically worked to free myself from this potential hazard, the force of the waves and the draw of the currents were so powerful that the only way to even hope to keep my head above water was with the help of the life jacket—I know that I could not have survived without it.

As the overturned boat exited the rapids and began to swirl in a side eddy, a few of us worked together to flip the boat upright so our guide could navigate it to the beach. Once on land, we rested and shared our individual experiences and feelings.

So what does this have to do with agency, marriage, and divorce? Both my wife and I chose willingly to go on this adventure—neither of us was pressured in any way. We knew beforehand that there would be risks and challenges, although we could not imagine how intense and frightening the actual time in the rapids would be. We gained great assurance from the skill and experience of our guides and the knowledge that a boat-flipping was a very rare event. We were properly prepared for the dangers—we heeded the training and requirement to wear approved life jackets, properly installed. We do not know for sure what caused the boat to flip. Had we known, we may have prevented it—but it is history now and we cannot change it. Once we were in the water, if I could have seen or found my wife, I would have tried to help her, but the only thing I could do while in the rapids was try to stay alive and help those I could see. After we had rested and regained control of the boat, we then approached Big Drop III with much more experience and caution than previously applied (even though we were cautious always—but now we were cautious at a higher level of experience).[3]

We each have the absolute gift of personal agency and are free to choose whether or not to accept and live the gospel of Jesus Christ. We each choose whether or not we will marry. We are free to attempt to persuade and lead others to follow Christ, but we cannot force anyone to believe as we believe. The deepest yearnings of our soul may have positive influence with another, but God will not allow circumvention of one person's agency for the enhancement of another's. We may bind ourselves together by vows and covenants, but we continue in the retention of our individual agency. Hearts may change. We may work really hard to be worthy of and to influence the love of another toward us, but we can never force it. Love is a positive affirmation of individual choice.

If someone who knew of my described river adventure were to ask my advice about taking such a trip themselves, I could offer much helpful advice (probably beginning with, "Do not go"). But if I could only tell them one thing, it would be, "Wear your life jacket in the whitewater!" If I could only offer one statement of counsel about the journey of our mortal lives, I would say, "Wear your fine linen—it is your spiritual life jacket!" Let me explain.

In the Revelation of John, one of the most hoped-for high events of all time is described—even the marriage supper of the Lamb. Christ as the Bridegroom has prepared the way for His bride—the righteous Saints—to be united with Him in eternal glory forever in the kingdom of the Father. John states, "Let us be glad and rejoice, and give honour to him: for the marriage of the Lamb is come, and his wife hath made herself ready. And to her was granted that she should be arrayed in fine linen, clean and white: *for the fine linen is the righteousness of saints*. And he saith unto me, Write, Blessed are they which are called unto the marriage supper of the Lamb. And he saith unto me, These are the true sayings of God" (Revelation 19:7–9; emphasis added).

The key to binding our eternal, God-given potential to our mortal, fallen lives and choices, then, is to use our glorious gift of agency to don the fine linen of righteousness—"to choose liberty and eternal life, through the great Mediator of all men" (2 Nephi 2:27). We cannot choose for another, but we can choose for ourselves. And as we righteously do so, we may better influence and help others in making correct choices.

And although agency is a divine, eternal gift, we are accountable for how we use it. If we misuse it, we will be held responsible before God. The First Presidency has taught this in relation to families in particular: "We warn that individuals who violate covenants of chastity, who abuse spouse or offspring, or who fail to fulfill family responsibilities will one day stand accountable before God."[4]

I have long appreciated the counsel of Joseph Smith as he dismissed the members of Zion's Camp after they were unable to complete their desired objectives:

> But thus it is: what men and great movements might attain to is often defeated, sometimes by the actions of enemies, sometimes by the lack of devotion and faith and energy on the part of those into whose hands great enterprises are committed. While God's general purposes will never ultimately be defeated by man, still upon each side of the general purposes of God a margin somewhat wide seems to have been left in which those both for and against those purposes may write what history they please—one that will meet with the approval of God, or one that will meet only with condemnation—herein is the agency of man. But in the exercise of that agency God's purposes will not be thwarted, for man's agency will not extend so far as that; if it did, it would interfere with God's agency and decrees.[5]

If you want to heal from divorce, it is necessary to properly understand the interplay between our agency and the agency of others. We must learn to honor the agency of others. God does. He allows our companions to deceive us, mistreat us, fall out of love with us, break their promises with us, and divorce us if they so please.

We must also learn to honor our own agency and to accept the consequences thereof. We may choose to repent of our sins—or not. We may choose to love and serve those who do not love us—or not. We may choose to forgive others—or not. We may choose to pick ourselves up from the ashes of our broken lives—or not. Once we come to understand and appreciate the priceless gift of our agency and how to properly exercise it to effect our promise of eternal life, we are then free to experience the healing of our broken hearts.

Notes

1. Robert D. Hales, "'Come, Follow Me' by Practicing Christian Love and Service," *Ensign*, Nov. 2016.
2. At the point of traversing the three major rapids, our two children were in a different boat than us and made it through without incident. They later jokingly complained that they had been cheated out of the full adventure.
3. One of my life mottos is *Good judgment comes from experience. Experience comes from poor judgment.* I do not know the original source of this statement, but when I heard it, I adopted it as my own.
4. "The Family: A Proclamation to the World," *Ensign*, Nov. 2010, 129.
5. Joseph Smith Jr, *History of the Church of Jesus Christ of Latter-day Saints*, ed. B. H. Roberts (Salt Lake City: The Church of Jesus Christ of Latter-day Saints, 1909), 2:123.

Four

Forgive All

One of my goals when teaching the gospel has been to give simple explanation and illustration of important principles. For example, I loved to teach the Lord's law of forgiveness in a simple way. Often many years after our class, I have asked a former student if they can explain the law. It is sweet when the reply is, "Forgive All."

Here is how we did it. I made a poster with a large blank space and a caption, "The Lord's Law of Forgiveness?" I then told the students that we would discuss this important law and illustrate it on our poster to better help us remember it. We then discussed the context and background of the verse that states, "I, the Lord, will forgive whom I will forgive, but of you it is required to forgive all men" (D&C 64:10). Next we discussed how we could complete our poster to illustrate the principle. After a bit of discussion—with occasional need for a prompt—some student would say, "We could attach a box of *ALL* laundry detergent to the blank space of the poster." (By then, they were well acquainted with my many posters and object lessons.) I then presented to them just such a box that I had prepared in advance. As the students saw the poster hanging in the classroom for the balance of the year, with its colorful, big, bold "*ALL*," they experienced regular, simple reminders of this very important principle. We had the added blessing of also seeing the slogan printed on the box: "Fights the toughest stains."

Perhaps you are the victim of physical and mental abuse from your former spouse. Perhaps even other family members and acquaintances have mistreated you, not understanding the true nature of what you have suffered. Perhaps you have been mistreated by civic authorities who decreed your divorce, or maybe you have been judged unfairly by a spiritual leader who failed to grasp your condition. In all of these scenarios and many more, there is an ultimate standard that God expects of you—Forgive All!

Perhaps you are dealing with a hypocrite. If so, remember the Lord's law of the hypocrite as given in modern revelation: "But the hypocrites shall be detected and shall be cut off, either in life or in death, even as I will" (D&C 50:8). We let the Lord deal with the hypocrites in His due time—our task is to Forgive All!

Perhaps you have been the perpetrator of contention and abuse toward your former spouse on a scale large or small. Perhaps you have been in denial of your sins and sought to gloss them over, using the human weaknesses of others as some sort of excuse or alibi for your own unchristian behavior. Whatever your condition, there is an ultimate standard that God expects of you—Forgive All! (And that charge includes the forgiving of self, such forgiveness coming as an outgrowth of true repentance—the topic of an upcoming chapter.)

Perhaps in our human, fallen nature we may well struggle with distinguishing our role from that of our Savior: "I, the Lord, will forgive whom I will forgive." We may consciously or subconsciously think, "Oh yes, that is how I want to apply the law of forgiveness—on my own timetable and terms and only after my assailant has suffered much and fully repented." The Lord rescues us from our own flawed thinking by commanding that we *forgive all* and leave everyone else to Him and to His divine justice and mercy.

I once counseled a man who was going through a troubling divorce, forfeiting his peace of mind by seeking revenge against the injustice that seemed to be his. A simple analogy came to my mind, and as I shared it, I felt we connected. I asked: if he were to be bitten by a venomous snake, would his life and the lives of his children be better served by chasing after and killing the snake, or by seeking medical attention to heal his bite? Our Savior offers us the gift of healing. As we act to accept of His gift, we come to better understand His truth: "For my yoke is easy, and my burden is light" (Matthew 11:30).

Years ago I was prompted toward a study that helped me better understand why it is our Savior, and not us, who must be the one to "forgive whom I will forgive." As I was preparing one of my early manuscripts for publication, I used the phrase "unconditional love" in my effort to describe how our Savior deals with us. As my manuscript went through a blind peer review, my reviewer took the time to expound the doctrine of God's *divine*—but not unconditional—love for us. I reviewed several scriptural explanations of the "if" conditions required to receive the full and eternal benefit of God's love. For example, Jesus taught, "If ye keep my commandments, ye shall abide in my love; even as I have kept my Father's commandments, and abide in his love" (John 15:10). Another scripture records, "If you keep not my commandments, the love of the Father shall not continue with you, therefore you shall walk in darkness" (D&C 95:12). If we desire eternal life, or the type of life God enjoys, there are conditions we must meet.

Elder Russell M. Nelson taught the following:

> God declared that His work and glory is 'to bring to pass the immortality and eternal life of man.' Thanks to the Atonement, the gift of immortality is *unconditional*. The greater gift of eternal life, however, is *conditional*. In order to qualify, one must deny oneself of ungodliness and honor the ordinances and covenants of the temple. The resplendent bouquet of God's love—including eternal life—includes blessings for which we must qualify, not entitlements to be expected unworthily. Sinners cannot bend His will to theirs and require Him to bless them in sin. If they desire to enjoy every bloom in His beautiful bouquet, they must repent.[1]

God thus unburdens us by commanding that we forgive all. We are not obligated to carry the weight of other people's sins. He assumes that burden by His Atonement and He knows, with His divine and perfect love, how to help everyone strive for eternal life.

Now that we have discussed the doctrine *Forgive All*, what are we to do about it? We are to forgive all, obviously, but that is likely much easier said than done. Some of us may receive the gift of instant forgiveness—others may struggle through a long process for months and years. The main thing is that we keep at it until it happens. Fortunately we are blessed with many examples that can guide us in our quest. I will share two of my favorites—one an example of instant forgiveness and one of a soul who struggled longer-term. Both stories may inspire us and both certainly teach us true principles.

Forgiveness Is My Gift from God

When our son was in sixth grade, he came home one day with a story of an interesting visitor to his school, Jackie. As our son told us her story, my heart was touched and I desired to meet and talk with Jackie. I received her contact information from the school and when I called her, she kindly consented to meet with me and tell me her story.

Jackie, a few years previous, had been visiting a friend. While the friend was at work, Jackie was out in the yard and had heard a noise in the garage. As she entered the garage, she surprised two teenage boys who were in the process of stealing her car. The boys took her into the house and had her lie face down on the living room floor. After some discussion, they made a decision to shoot her, which they did—point blank in the back of the head with a .22 caliber pistol. The boys stole her car, abandoned and torched it in a vacant lot, and were apprehended before the day was over.

Jackie's friend returned home and found her within fifteen minutes of the shooting. She was rushed by life flight to the university hospital where she was stabilized. Although her family was told that she had only a two percent chance of living, she lived. She spent the next forty-five days in a coma. Her family was told that if she did survive, she would be nothing more than a "human vegetable" and that they should be looking for a nursing home for her. She, with her incredible faith and indomitable spirit, proved the doctors wrong. She emerged from her coma, miraculously recovered, and took charge of her life. She learned to live independently. Although she spoke and walked haltingly, she filled her life with good and positive activity. She retained her bright sense of humor and positive outlook on life. She began writing a book of her trials and willingly traveled many places to tell her story of faith and forgiveness.

Jackie contacted the young men who had committed the crime against her and regularly visited them in prison. She developed a particularly close relationship with the one who did the shooting. She forgave him! She told me that she now loves him as she does her own sons. I was so touched by her story that I invited her to come and speak to our institute students. She graciously consented. What follows are excerpts from the talk she gave to our students and from my personal interview with her:

- "I have forgiven my attackers. I forgave them as soon as they committed the crime. I did it for myself. I did it so my life could go forward."
- "People, when they hear that I forgive them, say that I must have a head injury. I do have a head injury—I have six bullet fragments in my head."
- "'How can you forgive?' people ask. It is easy—I wanted to get on with my life. It meant forgiving and I did forgive. I forgive—I don't forget."
- "The principle of forgiveness is something I have always had. It is my gift from God. I can laugh because I can forgive. I can forgive. I can love. It is my gift that I will now give to them [her attackers]."
- "It is easier for me to forgive than to hold a grudge. I want to go on with my life."[2]

JOHN, LEAVE IT ALONE

On at least two occasions in general conference, I have heard President Boyd K. Packer tell a powerful story of forgiveness. He told of his association with an elderly patriarch and former mission president he calls "John" whom he described as "saintly." President Packer did not guess of John's early-life trial until one evening when John told his story. When John was a young man, he had worked hard to make a good life for himself and his new wife. He gained an education and was soon well employed; they were expecting their first baby. When the time for the baby's birth arrived, there were serious complications and the only doctor in the community was out in the country attending to the sick. When summoned, he came as soon as he could, acted quickly in good faith, and the mother and baby were spared.

Then tragedy struck—some days after the birth of the baby, the young mother died from an infection carried to her by the doctor from another patient he had been treating on the day that he had come to attend to her. John was devastated, heartbroken, and angry. He blamed the doctor for his negligence and felt that he should be banned from his medical practice. He carried the burden forward week after week. President Packer speaks as follows:

> One night a knock came at his door. A little girl said simply, "Daddy wants you to come over. He wants to talk to you."

"Daddy" was the stake president. A grieving, heartbroken young man went to see his spiritual leader.

This spiritual shepherd had been watching his flock and had something to say to him.

The counsel from that wise servant was simply, "John, leave it alone. Nothing you do about it will bring her back. Anything you do will make it worse. John, leave it alone."

My friend told me then that this had been his trial—his Gethsemane. How could he leave it alone? Right was right! A terrible wrong had been committed and somebody must pay for it. It was a clear case.

But he struggled in agony to get hold of himself. And finally, he determined that whatever else the issues were, he should be obedient.

Obedience is powerful spiritual medicine. It comes close to being a cure-all.

He determined to follow the counsel of that wise spiritual leader. He would leave it alone.

Then he told me, "I was an old man before I understood! It was not until I was an old man that I could finally see a poor country doctor—overworked, underpaid, run ragged from patient to patient, with little medicine, no hospital, few instruments, struggling to save lives, and succeeding for the most part.

"He had come in a moment of crisis, when two lives hung in the balance, and had acted without delay.

"I was an old man," he repeated, "before I finally understood! I would have ruined my life," he said, "and the lives of others."

Many times he had thanked the Lord on his knees for a wise spiritual leader who counseled simply, "John, leave it alone."[3]

Our Savior, who loves us with an eternal, divine, abiding love, gives us the same charge: *Forgive All!* As we find the strength, the path, and the courage to do so in all matters related to our divorce and to our life, we will find that we are well on our way to having our broken hearts mended.

Notes

1. Russell M. Nelson, "Divine Love," *Ensign*, Feb. 2003; emphasis in original.
2. This experience of Jackie Millar happened near her home (and ours) of Madison, Wisconsin, a few decades previous to the time of this writing.
3. Boyd K. Packer, "Balm of Gilead," *Ensign*, Nov. 1987.

Five

Eternal Sociality

Occasionally when my daughter calls and asks what I am doing, I reply, "Oh, I am at lunch (or on a hike, or whatever) with my BFF" (Best Friend Forever). She knows to reply, "Oh, so you are dining alone today." And then we laugh.

I feel that one of my personal blessings is contentment in solitude. Some of this contentment has come through my profession of coordinating seminaries and institutes of religion throughout my state. I would often teach and visit classes and conduct training meetings with teachers or priesthood leaders—but because my area was large, I would generally only be able to get to one or sometimes two such events in a day. I would then set up my traveling office in the nearest chapel and spend most of the day alone in my administrative duties, study, and preparation for classes and meetings. I also spent countless hours driving alone, my car becoming a quiet refuge of peace.

Much of my progress toward personal contentment—though difficult—has come from my experience with divorce. This "imposed aloneness" has, in a sense, forced my hand in seeking greater peace and comfort through personal prayer, scripture study, temple attendance, life planning, writing of my personal history, and other activities.

I would counsel anyone going through divorce to learn to cherish your time alone. As you learn to process the heartache and loneliness—much of it not pleasant or peaceful—you may find increased opportunities to engage in thorough and sincere introspection about your eternal self. One of the most profound doctrines of our theology is the eternal nature of our soul. Our life experience consists of our premortal, our mortal, and our eternal life realms. As we are born, we bring forward our character and spirit from our premortal life. As we live out our mortal lives and make our life choices, we chart our course for eternity. We are each born once, we die once, and we are resurrected once. We do not reincarnate as something or someone else. We are not annihilated at death—we live forever, so we may as well get used to the notion and learn to love our eternal selves. Out of our trials and dark days, we may find great opportunities for progress—times to learn and grow and repent and develop our self-confidence and chart a true forward course. We learn that every good choice we make enhances our peace and joy in life.

In learning to better understand ourselves, we may take the words of William Shakespeare as a guide, "This above all: to thine own self be true, / And it must follow, as the night the day, / Thou canst not then be false to any man."[1]

But there is a flip side of contentment in solitude—delighting in our friendships. I began this book with sharing some of my deepest fears and feelings at my newly divorced status. I recounted some of the recurring questions of my troubling thoughts—What are people saying and thinking? Why am I so embarrassed at my status? Why am I avoiding people who have been my truest friends?

As I journeyed forward in my new status, I did encounter a few people who seemed to unjustly judge and perhaps a few who seemed to exhibit a holier-than-thou attitude about divorce, but, to my joy, nearly all the people I personally interacted with were genuine, kind, empathetic, and sincere in their efforts to offer understanding and support. I have been inspired by the former friendships that were enhanced and the new friendships that developed since my divorce.

Years ago, if you had asked me how many people had positively influenced my life, I would have said, "probably a few hundred." Now, partly through an enhanced perspective from my involvement with social media, my answer is, "thousands and counting." I treasure my family, my childhood friends, my school classmates, my mission and military associates, my work colleagues, my neighbors, my former students, my fellow service volunteers, and many others. I have been ministered to by many eternal friends.

At the time of my divorce, I was transitioned into the staff of the Human Resources department at the Church Office Building for several months. I was assigned to work on a project with a man about a decade older than I. He had much life experience in the world of business and had then come to work for the Church. He was wise and well-seasoned in life. Almost miraculously, we formed an immediate rapport and spent many delightful hours together in our work and lunch breaks. He seemed to know everyone and introduced me to one and all as we moved about. He had the gift to look into my soul, and he offered me wise and prudent counsel. He spoke very plainly to me with pragmatic wisdom, and I accepted it as from the true friend he was. I am so grateful for his time with me, and I look forward to continuing our friendship throughout eternity.

A long-time friend I met in junior high school and his wife and family made a special effort to reach out to me. They invited me to their home for dinner. They called me. They visited me. They reached out to my children. They reminded me of my positive potential and helped keep me grounded in gospel truth. They delighted in my remarriage and welcomed my new wife, Carol, into their home and hearts. We have traveled together. We were already good friends, but our time together during my trial enhanced our friendship. In proper due time, I long for our postmortal lives so we can hopefully spend more time together with our eternal friends.

Each of the several men who have been my bishop since the divorce have been marvelous ministers and have blessed my life and the lives of my family. They have seemed to sense when I could be blessed by a lunch outing or an interview or an informal chat as we cross paths. I honor and trust the mantle that guides their inspiration. I recall one particular occasion when I had walked from my institute office to visit my bishop on the university campus. After our business, he took the initiative to engage in personal conversation with me and he discerned that I was hurting. He directly counseled me and then simply asked, "Would you like a blessing?" and then gave me a powerful, inspired blessing of hope and comfort.

On another occasion with another bishop, I sought formal counsel through a scheduled interview. I was gratified as I discovered that he had done his homework, having studied doctrines and made preparation to give me direct, inspired counsel. He discussed with me an inspired prophetic quotation that has become a personal guiding gem of wisdom ever since. I am grateful beyond expression for the Lord's system of lay-ministry guidance from inspired leaders who live and work in the real world and then consecrate their time in giving inspired ministry to those under their stewardship. I feel an eternal connection to each of these great leaders and look forward to everlasting friendship with them.

Hopefully our family members are among our truest friends. In my case, my sister and my sister-in-law particularly looked after me. They visited me, counseled me, guided me, and sometimes gave me strong direction that I could not seem to fully grasp for myself. And of course I needed to make my own decisions—and sometimes the counsel given was not exactly what I desired or chose in the end—but it was a beginning and it kept me moving in the right direction, bringing me ultimate desired blessings. I knew that I could trust my family to give me true guidance and support.

A friend I met in college had gone through the trials of divorce some years before my trial. He understood. Although his and every circumstance is unique, he knew the principles needed to heal and move forward. He kept in touch with me. He understood my aloofness during times I could not bring myself to connect with him or our group of friends. He found ways to help. Specifically, he has taken time on multiple occasions to write me long, detailed letters in which he reminded me who I was and what my gifts and talents were. He pointed me toward the guiding light at the end of the tunnel of despair. He gave me hope. When I first met him and others of the college-days era of my life, I was inexperienced and naïve enough to think that once we parted company to follow our own life paths, we would permanently disconnect and drift away. Now with many decades of experience and understanding behind me, I cannot imagine not having this good man and so many others as my eternal friends.

When I was young and newly married, I served as counselor to a dedicated bishop. His wife worked with me in my profession. They knew, loved, and encouraged our growing family. When we divorced, they were heartbroken. They reached out with love and service. They spoke plainly of matters of life and encouraged me to go forward. They rejoiced in my healing and progress. When I think of them, I joy in so much history together. We have often reminisced of the good times we had with our ward members as we camped on our family farm property, and we have tried to imagine together the joy we will feel someday when we can gather once again in the eternal realm and laugh and reflect on the richness of our lives and friendships.

I have shared these examples knowing full well that they are representative of so many others. I am so blessed and so grateful for my true, eternal friendships.

I counsel everyone, and particularly those suffering through divorce, to take pause and ponder the history and richness of your friendships. Nurture them. Embrace them. Savor them. And do not feel guilty about the time your friends invest in your well-being. Their love of and service to you will not bless *only* your life—it will bless theirs. King Benjamin's charge "to love one another and to serve one another" implies a two-way street (Mosiah 4:15). Of course, we are to be sensitive to the needs and time constraints of our friends, but it would be folly to reject their sincere offers of help because of fear of imposing upon them. True friends offer true help and service. Accept them.

Just as every right choice we make brings us closer to eternal life, every right connection we make with our friends enriches our eternal sociality with them. All are blessed therefrom. The more of life that I live, and the more I interact with my friends, the more profound this scripture becomes for me, "And that same sociality which exists among us here will exist among us there, only it will be coupled with eternal glory, which glory we do not now enjoy" (D&C 130:2).

Note

1. William Shakespeare, "Hamlet," Act 1 Scene III.

Six

Keep in Remembrance

Shortly after I received my driver's license as a young man, a friend of mine sustained permanent disabilities from a car-train accident. This incident shook me and reinforced a cardinal rule of driving that I was sure I would always remember—*Never drive a vehicle across a train track unless you have a clear space for your car on the other side of the track.* A few years ago, a friend had her car ripped in half by a train but fortunately and miraculously escaped serious injury. Once again, I was reminded of this basic rule.

Just one week ago from the time of this writing, my wife, a passenger, and I were driving back to the Jerusalem Center from our assignment in the Bethlehem branch. Shortly after we passed the old city of Jerusalem, we came to a complicated intersection of several odd-angle lanes of traffic plus two tracks for the commuter trains. As the light turned green, I drove through, only to find myself stopped exactly between the two tracks, the back of my car protruding into the path of one track and the front of the car into the other—with no clear space in front of me. And then came frightening panic as I noticed two trains coming our way from opposite directions. Fortunately, the space behind our car was clear and I was able to quickly back up and prevent serious accident and injury.

I knew absolutely in my heart and mind, from logic and experience, the value of the train track rule herein described. I have remembered and applied this rule countless times in my years of driving. I have taught it to others. But in a careless, distracted moment, I put myself and my loved ones at risk simply because I did not keep this rule in my remembrance.

In a metaphorical sort of way, divorce can be like driving out into a crowded intersection and then discovering that trains are coming at you from multiple directions. We do not expect to ever be in such peril, and now that we are, we wonder how and why we got there. The fearsome awesomeness of it all, to one degree or another, may cause us to forget the Lord. We must keep Him in our remembrance. It is He who will get us to safety from the oncoming trains of our divorce. I will share just a couple of ways we can remember Him and His guidance in our lives.

Journaling

Many years ago, when I served as a branch president at the Missionary Training Center in Provo, Utah, I had a young elder who called and arranged to visit with me early one Sunday morning. He shared with me how discouraged he was and how he felt that he was not progressing as he felt he should. He felt very inadequate compared to all of the other missionaries who seemed to be better at learning the language and teaching the gospel. I felt a simple flash of inspiration and asked him if he had kept a missionary journal. He replied that he had done so diligently since before his arrival on his mission. I gave him an assignment, telling him, "Elder, between now and our sacrament meeting this afternoon, I would like you to find a quiet place and read and ponder every word you have written in your journal."

When the elder entered our sacrament meeting, he was happy and smiling. His countenance had brightened. His welcome comment to me was, "President, I guess I am doing better than I thought I was." I could have told him that but wanted him to hear it in his own words from his own record. I wanted him to remember his own life and how the Lord had blessed him in his preparation and his mission.

I counsel everyone—and particularly those of us dealing with the trial of divorce—to keep a sacred record of our lives by whichever of the many available methods we may choose. As we do so, and then occasionally read and review what we have recorded, we remember that the Lord is with us and that, through our trials, there is constant guidance and spiritual direction being consistently poured out upon us. In addition to helping us see where we have come from, writing can focus our thoughts and feelings and give us powerful insight for moving forward.

In our first ward after college, my former wife and I were invited to attend a family history class. The instructor inspired me to keep a personal history, so I began collecting memorabilia of my life and storing it in a cardboard box where it remained for the next twenty years with not much further action. But a seed had been planted in my soul that would, in due time, germinate and grow into something I am now very grateful for.

Our instructor shared a quotation from President Spencer W. Kimball that became a motivating and guiding star for the writing of my personal history: "Those who keep a book of remembrance are more likely to keep the Lord in remembrance in their daily lives. Journals are a way of counting our blessings and of leaving an inventory of these blessings for our posterity."[1]

Ironically enough, my time for action in actually writing my personal history came with my call to serve as bishop of my ward. I had some flexibility with my summer schedule and made plans to go with the youth on all of their campouts. During these outings, I had many free hours and found a quiet place to work. I first organized my life into five-year time periods and then organized my life events into somewhat of a chronological list within each of the periods. I then began writing. As I did not have many computer skills or access to a computer out in the wild, I wrote longhand on legal pads. I then hired my teenage son to do the word processing for me and, before long, had several printed and hardbound copies of the first volume for members of my family. In the ensuing years, with the addition of a computer and acquired skills, I have done my own writing and processing. I have included a photocopy section in each volume for special letters, notes, news articles, etc. I currently have four bound volumes and a fifth open-ended electronic volume that is constantly in progress.

Through this process of writing my personal history, I have learned the truth of President Kimball's promise about keeping the Lord in remembrance. Through the process of writing, editing, and revisiting my personal history, I see very clearly the hand of the Lord in my life. I see the thread of my testimony of truth intermingling with and connecting together the events of my life.

Specific to my divorce, as difficult and terrible at it was, I now have enough pre- and post-divorce life history to help me place and keep it in proper perspective. I better understand who I am—a son of Heavenly Parents, with long premortal and mortal evidence of striving to be in favor with God and to be worthy of His blessings. I now have many years of learning of and preparing for an eternal life of continued blessings and renewal. Although my divorce, at the time, seemed like driving into a train wreck, with the passage of time and reminders of Heavenly Father's guidance during that time, it is seeming now more like a bump in the road—a serious bump, but not a fatal one as I supposed it would be at the time.

As you can likely surmise, personal history has become a life passion and a serious hobby for me. It need not be such for you for it to still be profoundly helpful. Perhaps a simple listing of your lifelong talents, strengths, and blessings received from the Lord is all you would need to be able to see and remember your successful life and the Lord's constant guiding hand throughout.

Sacrament Meeting

I believe that, as we properly prepare for and participate in sacrament meeting, we may come to always keep the Lord and His goodness in our memory and in our daily life activities. Looking back, my experiences with sacrament meeting have been some of the most encouraging and helpful events for enduring my trials.

When I served as bishop, I was invited to join with stake presidents and bishops of many stakes of our region in a Sunday afternoon solemn assembly in the Salt Lake Temple. Shortly after we were all seated in a large assembly room, the First Presidency and all members of the Quorum of the Twelve Apostles entered the room, all dressed in white. They then conducted a sacrament meeting with members of the Twelve blessing and administering the sacrament to us. Several then instructed us in the important issues of our ministry, including the proper conducting of sacrament meetings in our wards.

In the weeks following our special meeting, our stake president led us in discussion of ways we could improve the sacrament meeting worship among our members. Over the coming months, we trained our leaders and taught our ward members how to enhance their spiritual growth through sacrament meeting. I hope our efforts were helpful to them in drawing closer to the Lord and remembering Him and His promises in their lives. But I know for sure what the whole experience did for me personally. I have learned that as I make the effort to arrive early, lay aside personal business and conversation as I enter the chapel, and focus on reverence and sacred music to prepare for the crowning ordinance of the sacrament, my experience is enhanced. As it turned out, the comfort, remembrance, and growth I experienced in my renewed efforts at proper sacrament meeting participation became a spiritual life preserver for me just a few years later during the trial of my divorce.

Worthily partaking of the sacrament is all about remembering our Savior, what He has done for us, and what we covenant to do that we may receive the full effect of His Atonement in our lives. Summary of our task is sublimely stated in our sacrament prayers: "That they may eat in remembrance of the body of thy Son, and witness unto thee, O God, the Eternal Father, that they are willing to take upon them the name of thy Son, and always remember him and keep his commandments which he has given them; that they may always have his Spirit to be with them. Amen" (D&C 20:77).

From our pondering of this statement, we are reminded that we have an Eternal Father who has a beautiful plan and mission for us and who has given us His Son as our Savior and Redeemer. It is important for us to attend sacrament meeting each week so we are less likely to become distracted and less likely to forget our Savior and His saving power. Forgetting means putting ourselves in peril from the approaching trains of destruction that could disrupt our peace and happiness.

Through our weekly sacrament meeting worship, and in particular the partaking of the emblems of the sacrament, we renew our covenant that we will remember the Atonement and keep the commandments given us by our Savior. As we humbly and sincerely accomplish the renewal of our covenants, we grow in understanding that such covenants are not in the least restrictive but actually liberate us from our pain and suffering and allow us to come again into the glorious light and peace of mind available to us.

As we consistently observe the Sabbath and the renewal of our covenants through our partaking of the sacrament, we receive the consummate gift of the pure guidance of the Holy Ghost throughout our lives—"that they may always have his Spirit to be with them." With deep gratitude, I remember the countless times this gift has blessed me—has warned me of danger and shown me an escape route from destructive forces trying to ruin my life.

I have received specific guidance from the Holy Ghost during the trial of my divorce. I hope the guidance I share will prompt your memory of your own guidance received and testify of the truth and power of the principle and promise of worthily attending sacrament meeting and partaking of the sacrament.

I was guided in my life course—where to go, what to do, and how to achieve my goals. Countless times I was blessed with enough peace of mind to see me through the hour or the day. I was often prompted to attend the temple where peace and spiritual light were given to me, where I sometimes interacted with kind and wise souls who counseled me in correct principles and actions. I received promptings of how to serve in my church callings. My mind was expanded to include ways I could use my God-given gifts to bless the lives of others. Many times, I have received inspiration of specific things I could write or speak to help others who were hurting.

I was strongly prompted that I was to walk away from any contentious court battle that would have just made things worse for my family and me. I received a very clear impression that, even though instant forgiveness did not seem to be my gift, the choice to forgive would bless my life and the lives of others. Often I have felt what I should say or do to help my children in their struggles with the divorce of their parents. Many times, I have been given enough of a glimpse of eternal life to help keep me motivated and moving forward.

Although I feel I am often quite cognizant of current guidance from the Lord in my life, much of the help I have received has been quiet and subtle and perhaps not even recognized as promptings from the Spirit until well after the fact. I often see the hand of the Lord in my life more clearly in hindsight than in real time. But, gratefully, I feel I have come to know His guidance. And I know with absolute certainty that my life is much better because of the years of effort I have made to properly prepare for and worship in sacrament meeting—particularly in the partaking of the holy sacrament.

I hope the same for you: that you, too, can develop a fervent love for the time of sacred communion each week that you prepare for and partake of the sacrament. I pray that this will become a sacred time for you and that it will be a time of gaining strength and forward direction. I hope that you—whatever format and method you may choose—will be able to record your thoughts and feelings about your trials and successes and that such remembrances will serve as a reminder to you of the hand of the Lord in your life—past, present, and future.

Note

1. Edward L. Kimball, ed., *The Teachings of Spencer W. Kimball* (Salt Lake City: Bookcraft, 1982), 349.

SEVEN

Live in Thanksgiving

LET US PAUSE AND SUMMARIZE A FEW ESTABLISHED THEMES OF THIS writing so far. Even in the midst of our hard trial of divorce, we can find much to be grateful for. The focal point of our gratitude is Heavenly Father's great plan of happiness and our Savior's Atonement, which allows us redemption and access to that great plan, which leads us to eternal life. As we keep our eternal perspective, forgive others, properly use our gift of agency, and keep the Lord and His gospel in our remembrance, we come to know that obedience to the Lord's commandments is not restrictive, but liberating. He taught, "And ye shall know the truth, and the truth shall make you free" (John 8:32). Truth makes us totally free if we accept it and live it, if we obey the commandments given to us to guide us to eternal life. As we do so, we have much to be thankful for. We do well to demonstrate our gratitude by our obedience to the Lord's commandments.

I have thought much about the relationship between obedience and gratitude. I believe that each enhances and propels the other in an upward spiral. The more obedient we are to gospel truth, the more grateful we are for it. The more grateful we are for gospel truth, the more obedient we become to the truths we know.

As I served at the Missionary Training Center, a major aspect of our work was helping the missionaries learn to be obedient to the Lord and to the expectations of being missionaries. I often used my experience of Army basic training in an effort to help my missionaries understand our purpose. I shared with them how we kept our footlockers precisely organized and immaculately clean with our clothing and possessions all in order and displayed on a white towel. We then made the point that after basic training, the norm was different—a soldier in combat would not keep the same standard for his footlocker, but his life and the lives of others may depend on the lessons of obedience he had learned from the discipline of his basic training, exemplified by maintaining a neat locker.[1]

During my time of service at the Missionary Training Center, I was taught a great spiritual lesson by our newly called President Ed J. Pinegar. Concurrent with my efforts to teach the principle of obedience to the missionaries of my assigned branch, he was pondering and seeking revelation on the same matter for all of the missionaries of the MTC. I recall the day that he so excitedly shared with us and with the missionaries the result of his many weeks of seeking inspiration. He announced that he felt that "the key to obedience is gratitude." It was as sublime as it was simple.

As I considered the notion, pondered and studied application of it, and continued to be tutored by President Pinegar on the matter, I came to embrace the principle as my own. I now believe that a grand key to obedience is gratitude. I am convinced that we could choose any gospel principle at random and contemplate how our obedience to it is driven by our gratitude. For example, I do not pay tithing because it is some rule of my faith or so I can gain favor or praise from others. I doubt many people do in the long term. I pay tithing because I am grateful to my Heavenly Father for His plan and Church, and I want to see people throughout the world receive the same blessings I have received. I do not repent of my sins so I can check an item off of a list. I repent because I am grateful for the Atonement that allows me to be forgiven so I may feel peace with myself and with God and continue to strive for the life He offers. And so forth . . .

So how then do we increase our gratitude? There are more ways than we can likely imagine. I know a man who purchased a special clock that chimed each hour. He hung it in his business office and, at each chime, paused for just a moment to remember the Lord and His goodness to him. Another friend told me of his "thanksgiving prayer" tradition. Each Thanksgiving day, he spends several hours in prayer and meditation just enumerating and remembering his many blessings. And I am confident that he had a habit of thanksgiving all year long. (I also note that he was newly divorced at the time he shared this with me.) I often see activities on social media where people have accepted a particular challenge to post something each day for which they are grateful. A systematic study of gratitude and thanksgiving in the scriptures helps to focus our minds toward more gratitude. The methods are endless—we just need to find what works for us and do it.

There are several teachings illustrating the doctrine of gratitude found throughout the scriptures. In one of my favorite revelations on the topic, the Lord confirms the premise of the relationship between obedience and gratitude. He first reminds us of the glorious gift of eternal life that He offers to Heavenly Father's children:

> For those that live shall inherit the earth, and those that die shall rest from all their labors, and their works shall follow them; and they shall receive a crown in the mansions of my Father, which I have prepared for them. (D&C 59:2)

The Lord then confirms that His commandments are not restrictions upon our freedom but declares that they are rather "blessings" for us:

> And they shall also be crowned with blessings from above, yea, and with commandments not a few. (v. 4)

After reviewing some of His commandments, He reminds us to be grateful "in all things" (v. 7).

And He reasserts, as we have discussed, that sacrament meeting is where we commune with Him and receive our direction and blessings for our progress:

> And that thou mayest more fully keep thyself unspotted from the world, thou shalt go to the house of prayer and offer up thy sacraments upon my holy day. (v. 9)

Again He reminds us to be joyfully grateful:

> And inasmuch as ye do these things with thanksgiving, with cheerful hearts and countenances, not with much laughter, for this is sin, but with a glad heart and a cheerful countenance. (v. 15)

The Lord then continues to describe the blessing associated with this charge—the beautiful earth and the fullness thereof. Personally, I love to bask in the serenity of these verses and contemplate all that the Lord has done for us and all that He has given us:

> Verily I say, that inasmuch as ye do this, the fulness of the earth is yours, the beasts of the field and the fowls of the air, and that which climbeth upon the trees and walketh upon the earth;
>
> Yea, and the herb, and the good things which come of the earth, whether for food or for raiment, or for houses, or for barns, or for orchards, or for gardens, or for vineyards;
>
> Yea, all things which come of the earth, in the season thereof, are made for the benefit and the use of man, both to please the eye and to gladden the heart;
>
> Yea, for food and for raiment, for taste and for smell, to strengthen the body and to enliven the soul. (vs. 16–19)

In conclusion, the Lord reaffirms the need for gratefully acknowledging His blessings to us by our obedience:

> And it pleaseth God that he hath given all these things unto man; for unto this end were they made to be used, with judgment, not to excess, neither by extortion.
>
> And in nothing doth man offend God, or against none is his wrath kindled, save those who confess not his hand in all things, and obey not his commandments. (vs. 20–21)

In a different time and setting, the Lord gives us a powerful reminder of the need to be grateful and to acknowledge the source of our blessings. As He traveled through Samaria, ten lepers petitioned Him for healing. He obliged. Only one returned and gave thanks. (See Luke 17:15–16.)

Then the Lord asked the searching question:

> "Were there not ten cleansed? but where are the nine?" (v. 17)
>
> To the one who was grateful, the Lord reassured him of the reward for his faith and thankfulness:
>
> And he said unto him, Arise, go thy way: thy faith hath made thee whole. (v. 19)

Amulek taught the poor class of Zoramites—those who had been humbled by exclusion from their worship and their society—"that ye live in thanksgiving daily, for the many mercies and blessings which he doth bestow upon you" (Alma 34:38). I believe that to be excellent counsel for those of us hurting from and struggling through divorce—to "live in thanksgiving daily." Although we are suffering, we have the Lord's tender mercy and His bounteous blessings always with us. Sometimes we just need to find ways to enumerate them. We may receive great guidance from the inspired words of a familiar hymn:

> When upon life's billows you are tempest-tossed,
> When you are discouraged, thinking all is lost,
> Count your many blessings; name them one by one,
> And it will surprise you what the Lord has done.[2]

I have also found great guidance about gratitude outside of scripture. I have been inspired by a favorite poem for many years. A few decades ago when I first moved to Wisconsin, Carol and I were on a ride through the countryside near our home and passed a historical marker commemorating the birthplace of American author and poet Ella Wheeler Wilcox. That was the first time I realized that she was born in Wisconsin. In a small way, this new knowledge enamored her poem "Gethsemane" to me even more than it had been in the past. I had already loved it for several years.

> Gethsemane
>
> > In golden youth when seems the earth
> > A Summer-land of singing mirth,
> > When souls are glad and hearts are light,
> > And not a shadow lurks in sight,
> > We do not know it, but there lies
> > Somewhere veiled under evening skies
> > A garden which we all must see—
> > The garden of Gethsemane.
>
> With joyous steps we go our ways,
> Love lends a halo to our days;
> Light sorrows sail like clouds afar,
> We laugh, and say how strong we are.
> We hurry on; and hurrying, go
> Close to the border-land of woe,
> That waits for you, and waits for me—
> Forever waits Gethsemane.
>
> Down shadowy lanes, across strange streams,
> Bridged over by our broken dreams,
> Behind the misty caps of years,
> Beyond the great salt fount of tears,
> The garden lies. Strive as you may,

> You cannot miss it in your way.
> All paths that have been, or shall be,
> Pass somewhere through Gethsemane.
>
> All those who journey, soon or late,
> Must pass within the garden's gate;
> Must kneel alone in darkness there,
> And battle with some fierce despair
> God pity those who cannot say,
> 'Not mine but thine,' who only pray,
> 'Let this cup pass,' and cannot see
> The purpose in Gethsemane.[3]

The poem seems a bit open-ended and perhaps hints that each of us needs to seek out the purpose of our own Gethsemane. I have come to believe that the purpose of my own Gethsemane is to spend my lifetime in effort to attune my purpose with that of the Lord's—to declare to Him concerning my will, that it is not mine, but His. I believe that our universal life task is to exercise our will in doing His will—that we are to be grateful for His Atonement and demonstrate our gratitude by obeying His commandments. As we do so, He lifts us upward from our despair and sorrow to eternal peace and everlasting joy. The potential is worth our full effort. I am grateful for the prospect.

Notes

1. (Not relevant but just for fun.) President George Durrant was the president of the MTC who called me to serve and I was privileged to serve with him for a few months before his release. He was renowned for his quick wit. One day, I heard some missionaries complain to him about all of the rules of the MTC. "This place is like a prison," they lamented. He replied, "Oh no, elders, you do not understand. We are not at all like prison. If you were in prison, they would allow you to have visitors."
2. "Count Your Blessings," *Hymns*, no. 241.
3. Ella Wheeler Wilcox, *Poetical Works of Ella Wheeler Wilcox* (Edinburgh: W. P. Nimmo, Hay & Mitchell, 1917).

Eight

Ye Ought to Search the Scriptures

ALMA TAUGHT, "YE OUGHT TO SEARCH THE SCRIPTURES" (ALMA 33:2). Yes, we ought, but how and why? Many years ago, someone made a statement that resonated with me: "If you want to talk to God, pray. If you want Him to talk to you, read the scriptures." I later delighted when I heard Elder Robert D. Hales teach the same in general conference, "What a glorious blessing! For when we want to speak to God, we pray. And when we want Him to speak to us, we search the scriptures; for His words are spoken through His prophets. He will then teach us as we listen to the promptings of the Holy Spirit."[1] We are blessed when regular scripture study is a lifelong habit, and I believe it is especially essential to guide us through the dark challenges of divorce.

On many occasions, I have been invited to a youth conference or a Relief Society meeting or other function to teach the topic *How to Study the Scriptures*. I have assumed that these invitations have come because I was the seminary/institute instructor, feeling that the implication of the invitation has been that, because of my profession, I would have some elaborate method or some revolutionary plan for effectively studying the scriptures. I always hoped I would not disappoint by declaring that I knew of no such method that would have any sort of universal application.

When possible, I always accepted these invitations because I am a firm believer in scripture study. My approach was simple. I would share just a few of my personal study helps and then, rather than discuss methods, we would spend our time studying and discussing a block of scripture I felt was of particular application for the group. I am going to take the same approach in this chapter—I will share a few of my favorite simple methods, and then we will study the scriptures.

BROWN SUGAR PRINCIPLE

One of my fellow coordinators taught us what he called the "brown sugar" principle.[2] When I teach the principle to my students, I sometimes bring a pot of plain oatmeal to class. They are reluctant to eat and when I quiz them as to why, "bland" is a common descriptor of their hesitancy. When I then present some yummy additives to them, their attitude changes. Brown sugar seems to be a common favorite. We then discuss that sometimes we perceive the scriptures as bland, but if we are willing to "sweeten" them by searching for what we call "brown sugar words and phrases," the attitude and experience can improve. It is that simple—in our scripture study, we are blessed and helped by seeking for and pondering the doctrines that are sweet for us.

R.S.V.P.

At the very outset of my teaching career, the seminary and institute department adapted the French term "répondez s'il vous plaît" (R.S.V.P.) into a scripture study formula: "Read, Study, Visualize, and Ponder." In its simplicity, it was effective. Sometimes we may struggle with reading the scriptures because we are only *reading* the scriptures. When we really study them, trying to visualize the concepts and pondering the application and value of them to our lives, our understanding and edification increases.

Now let's study a scriptural passage. During the trying days and weeks right after my divorce, I was reading in the Book of Mormon of the account of the efforts of Alma and Amulek to teach, encourage, and reclaim the poor class of the Zoramites who had been cast out of their synagogues. All of the teachings associated with this occasion are wonderfully instructive and inspiring. For the sake of brevity in this writing, I will discuss only the final four verses of chapter thirty-four:

> That ye contend no more against the Holy Ghost, but that ye receive it, and take upon you the name of Christ; that ye humble yourselves even to the dust, and worship God, in whatsoever place ye may be in, in

> spirit and in truth; and that ye live in thanksgiving daily, for the many mercies and blessings which he doth bestow upon you.
>
> Yea, and I also exhort you, my brethren, that ye be watchful unto prayer continually, that ye may not be led away by the temptations of the devil, that he may not overpower you, that ye may not become his subjects at the last day; for behold, he rewardeth you no good thing.
>
> And now my beloved brethren, I would exhort you to have patience, and that ye bear with all manner of afflictions; that ye do not revile against those who do cast you out because of your exceeding poverty, lest ye become sinners like unto them;
>
> But that ye have patience, and bear with those afflictions, with a firm hope that ye shall one day rest from all your afflictions. (Alma 34:38–41)

Contend no more against the Holy Ghost: Divorce detours our life routine into strange and sometimes frightening pathways. Without the guidance of the Holy Ghost, we may lose our way. We contend against, or work in opposition to, the Holy Ghost when we do things we are not supposed to do or when we *don't* do things we are supposed to do. For example, if we are unwilling to forgive, we limit the power of the Holy Ghost to prompt and bless us. As we pray, study the scriptures and the words of the prophets, and seek to know the Lord's will in our lives, then we may have the constant companionship of the Holy Ghost to take us on our true path forward to the blessings the Lord has in store for us.

Take upon you the name of Christ: To take upon ourselves the name of Christ is to recognize that He is our *spiritual* father—the Father of our *salvation*. As we follow Him, He leads us to Heavenly Father and the blessings of eternal life He has promised us. We learn of what we must do as we listen to the living prophets who guide us in truth and righteousness. Abinadi taught:

> Behold I say unto you, that whosoever has heard the words of the prophets, yea, all the holy prophets who have prophesied concerning the coming of the Lord—I say unto you, that all those who have hearkened unto their words, and believed that the Lord would redeem his people, and have looked forward to that day for a remission of their sins, I say unto you, that these are his seed, or they are the heirs of the kingdom of God.

For these are they whose sins he has borne; these are they for whom he has died, to redeem them from their transgressions. And now, are they not his seed? (Mosiah 15:11–12)

Humble yourselves even to the dust: Divorce has a way of humiliating us and making us feel worthless, "even to the dust." The scriptures declare, "O how great is the nothingness of the children of men; yea, even they are less than the dust of the earth" (Helaman 12:7). Divorce can even do that—make us feel lower than dust. But the way we figuratively become "less than dust" is if we *do not* respond to and follow the commandments of Heavenly Father—because "dust" obeys Him. "For behold, the dust of the earth moveth hither and thither, to the dividing asunder, at the command of our great and everlasting God" (Helaman 12:8). The key to rising from the dust of our trials and walking the forward path is humble obedience to the will of God. He would not have us wallow in self-pity or doubt. His will is that we get up and get going in the management of our own lives and service to His children.

In being humbled by life, if we can become humble in the Lord's way—becoming as little children—He will guide us along:

> Verily, Verily, I say unto you, ye are little children, and ye have not as yet understood how great blessings the Father hath in his own hands and prepared for you;
>
> And ye cannot bear all things now; nevertheless, be of good cheer, for I will lead you along. The kingdom is yours and the blessings thereof are yours, and the riches of eternity are yours. (D&C 78:17–18)

Worship God, in whatsoever place ye may be in, in spirit and in truth: My divorce took me out of my family, my home, my ward, my stake, my profession, my community, and my state. But as I now consider all of the great experiences that I have had in places that were before strange to me, I cannot imagine life without the dear people I have met and the worshipful experiences I have had. I have met and worked with so many great souls from many religions and cultures that I fear I would not have met had I stayed in one place. And now our current immersion in the culture of the Holy Land through our service at the BYU Jerusalem Center is expanding my concept of and experience with worship in a broader scope than I had ever imagined. There are true and good people all over the world—many more, of course, than we hear of in the TV news. Within the Church, we may find true worship wherever we may go. And outside of the Church, we may find sincere people who are seeking truth and true worship in all parts of the planet. Truth is everywhere present if we wisely seek for it.

Live in thanksgiving daily: As discussed in the previous chapter, Amulek counsels us as to what we should be thankful for—"the many mercies and blessings which he doth bestow upon you" (Alma 34:38). I believe that, even though we may be suffering sorely and may be experiencing great loss in divorce, if we would and could count our many mercies and blessings, we would be awestruck with the goodness of the Lord in our lives—past, present, and future.

Be watchful unto prayer continually: Our already strong emotions and passions are accentuated by divorce. We may find ourselves more prone to anger, revenge, lust, sarcasm, self-doubt, discouragement—and a whole range of unhealthy and unproductive thoughts and feelings. Amulek's counsel can be our protective shield against such. As we try to continually seek spiritual guidance and help through our constant prayers, we have the promise "that ye may not be led away by the temptations of the devil, that he may not overpower you" (Alma 34:39). In another place, the Lord reaffirms the promise, "Pray always, that you may come off conqueror; yea, that you may conquer Satan, and that you may escape the hands of the servants of Satan that do uphold his work" (D&C 10:5).

Have patience, and bear with all manner of affliction: I was naïve at the time of my divorce in thinking, perhaps mostly subconsciously, that since I was suffering so much, I would be exempted from further major trials and heartaches. Since my profession was disrupted because of the divorce, I felt that the Lord would bless me with immediate temporal blessings. Since I had always desired marriage to a true and good companion, I felt that I would be led to such without much further trial. And so went my rationale.

I had misunderstood the Lord's tutoring timetable for my life. I had forgotten that His ways are not necessarily our ways, that He sees all in grand panorama and allows us to struggle so that we may learn and grow. And now, in hindsight, I clearly see and affirm that He has blessed me with all of the things here mentioned—He just did it on His terms and schedule and not on mine. And even when I felt that my desired blessings seemed to be eluding me, I now recognize that He was blessing me day by day with all that was needed to sustain me and to move me forward in pursuit of the righteous desires of my heart. His counsel to "have patience, and bear with those afflictions" is part of His grand plan for us. After enumerating a long list of the sufferings endured by Joseph Smith, the Lord reminded him, "The Son of Man hath descended below them all. Art thou greater than he?" (D&C 122:8). He knows what He is doing. We can trust Him.

Do not revile: In the Sermon on the Mount, Jesus taught, "Judge not, that ye be not judged" (Matthew 7:1). And yet, divorce is enfolded by judgment—some of it needful and legitimate, and some of it hurtful and unnecessary. Our task is to know the difference and act accordingly. The Joseph Smith Translation of the same scriptural verse helps immensely, "Judge not unrighteously, that ye be not judged; but judge righteous judgment." We need to rightly protect ourselves and our children from harm and danger, but, as previously discussed, we are to leave individual judgment of souls to God. Our task, along with rendering necessary righteous judgment, is to forgive.

Ye shall one day rest: The word *rest* is a super-sweet "brown sugar word" for me. The long emotional grind of divorce is strenuous and exhausting. In the scriptures, I have found hopeful relief in passages such as this from John the Revelator, "And God shall wipe away all tears from their eyes; and there shall be no more death, neither sorrow, nor crying, neither shall there be any more pain: for the former things are passed away" (Revelation 21:4).

And with another perspective, we add an additional layer of sweetness to the word *rest*. A respected teacher of mine once taught us to equate "rest" with "remainder" or "balance" in the sense that God has given us so much already and desires to give us the rest or the balance of what He has in store for us if we are faithful. The act of contemplating our future potential and considering our eternal destiny can be very comforting and motivating. It is refreshing and restful to our troubled souls to bask in "the hope of a glorious resurrection, through the grace of God the Father and his Only Begotten Son, Jesus Christ" (D&C 138:14).

"[We] ought to search the scriptures" (Alma 33:2). As we do so, seeking out the sweetness of the gospel through our study and pondering and as we read, study, visualize, and ponder, we hear God's individual messages to us, and we are well on the path of true and complete healing of our broken hearts.

Notes

1. Robert D. Hales, "Holy Scriptures: The Power of God unto Our Salvation," *Ensign*, Nov. 2006.
2. My friend Brother Todd Murdock was coordinating seminaries and institutes in Iowa City at the time I was doing so in Wisconsin. One year in our coordinator's conference, he shared this method with us. I immediately began to teach and apply it, and have loved it ever since.

Nine

Stand Blameless before God

President David O. McKay became the President of the Church just months before I was born, and he served as such until just months before I departed for my mission. I was saddened at his death and could not imagine anyone else as my prophet. But I did not have to imagine for long as our new President, Joseph Fielding Smith—already in his mid-nineties—came to visit us at the old Language Training Mission (LTM) on the Brigham Young University campus. He came with his wife, Jessie Evans Smith, and together they warmed our hearts and lifted our spirits with their testimonies and musical performances, including a piano duet, which he jokingly called a "Do It—because she told me I had to."

The highlight of President Smith's message for me was his sharing of the fourth section of the Doctrine and Covenants. He quoted it to us and then instructed us that if we wanted to be successful on our missions and in our lives, we should learn and live by this section of scripture:

> Now behold, a marvelous work is about to come forth among the children of men.
>
> Therefore, O ye that embark in the service of God, see that ye serve him with all your heart, might, mind and strength, that ye may stand blameless before God at the last day.
>
> Therefore, if ye have desires to serve God ye are called to the work;
>
> For behold the field is white already to harvest; and lo, he that thrusteth in his sickle with his might, the same layeth up in store that he perisheth not, but bringeth salvation to his soul;
>
> And faith, hope, charity and love, with an eye single to the glory of God, qualify him for the work.

> Remember faith, virtue, knowledge, temperance, patience, brotherly kindness, godliness, charity, humility, diligence.
> Ask, and ye shall receive; knock, and it shall be opened unto you. Amen. (D&C 4:1–7)

This passage is dripping with doctrine and ripe for endless pondering and application to our lives. Through the years I have often taught it with sweet remembrance of the day President Smith challenged us to live by it, but I must confess that my initial exuberance diminished in the complexity of life and the multitude of other life lessons to remember and apply.

But one day a few years after my divorce, remarriage, and subsequent reentry into my profession, I was talking with a beloved colleague about my heartaches for my family, and he took time to reteach me the fourth section of the Doctrine and Covenants. He focused his counsel on a single phrase: "that ye may stand blameless before God at the last day." He identified four aspects of being blameless and counseled with me about each, as summarized below.

Do Not Blame God

Did God orchestrate my divorce? No. Could He have prevented it, and if so, why didn't He? Perhaps—He can soften hearts and provide experiences for growth and choice in our lives, but He will not usurp our agency. Why did Shadrach, Meshach, and Abednego get a rescuing angel to deliver them from fire and Abinadi did not? I do not know, but trust that I will know better in the day when "all things shall be made known unto the children of men" (2 Nephi 30:16).

God could stop planes from crashing, fires from burning, earthquakes from shaking, murderers from killing, and floods from ravaging. But He does not always do so. I believe that He intervenes and assists in our lives—more often than we are even aware of. How and why and in what situations He chooses to do so will be better understood in the eternal realm. President Spencer W. Kimball taught:

> Could the Lord have prevented these tragedies? The answer is, Yes. The Lord is omnipotent, with all power to control our lives, save us pain, prevent all accidents, drive all planes and cars, feed us, protect us, save us from labor, effort, sickness, even from death, if he will. But he will

not. We should be able to understand this, because we can realize how unwise it would be for us to shield our children from all effort, from disappointments, temptations, sorrows, and suffering. The basic gospel law is free agency and eternal development. To force us to be careful or righteous would be to nullify that fundamental law and make growth impossible.[1]

In an informal setting, a general authority once shared with us of his responsibility to preside at the funeral service of a small child who had been killed in a tragic truck accident. During the service, innocently enough and in an effort to give comfort, some had taught the grieving parents that "God had called their son home" without realizing the pain and confusion this caused the young mother. "Why would God do this to us?" she probably wondered. As the final speaker, the general authority gently but clearly corrected the doctrine and taught that not every death or tragedy is God's will and doing. Not all who die are specifically called home. He told us that the young mother came to him after the service to thank him for his correction and to tell him that she could now see truth and begin to feel peace. She now felt better about God, knowing that He had not taken her son from her.

We do not always know the actions of God in our lives. We must not blame Him for the natural occurrences of our lives or the consequences of our choices. We do, however, always know that He is mindful of us, that He loves us, and that He will stand by us and comfort us and, in due time, heal our broken hearts.

Do Not Blame Others

When I was a young boy and would sometimes not share my toys or treats, my mother would scold me with "Don't be a dog in a manger"—a saying I grew up assuming was her original quip but is likely of ancient Greek origin. The imagery of the saying is of an ox or horse that tries to eat hay from a manger but is snapped at and prevented from doing so by a dog. The example was reinforced for me when I really saw a dog in the manger of our barn preventing one of our cows from eating the hay. The absurdity of the story is that the dog gains no value from hoarding the hay or grain—it is useless for him. The premise is, "If I can't have it, neither can you."

Sadly, many divorced couples play this dog-in-the-manger game for real, using each other and their children as pawns of their own misguided hurt and sorrow. At the time of this writing, I am aware of an actual, current dog-in-a-manger game sadly occurring with a young divorced mother engaged in attempting to disrupt the peace and happiness of her former husband and his new family. The sad irony is that the hurt she is causing is hurting her and her young child more than she realizes. She, and all who blame, would be much happier if they would allow the Lord to carry the burden and do His will with all people.

If we ever want our broken hearts to heal and gain full peace and joy, we need to get over blaming others for our own misfortune. True it is that the actions of others can hurt us and can cause us great mourning and sorrow, but healing comes when we leave their judgment to God.

Here is another scriptural gem that seemed to burst into my consciousness years ago, just at a time when I needed it the most. The context was a bit unexpected: the Lord is discussing the gifts of the Spirit and then at the end of a line about knowing the "differences of administration" is the declaration that He suits "his mercies according to the conditions of the children of men" (D&C 46:15).

Rather than blame others, let us leave their lives in the hands of our loving and all-knowing God, who knows even their premortal past, their mortal present, and their eternal potential. All are held accountable for their own sins—but only God knows the conditions and the degree of accountability to be measured out. Perhaps there are circumstances that, although they do not excuse a particular sin, may help explain it and may affect how God metes out justice and redemption. He who knows all conditions fairly administers His mercy.

Do Not Blame Yourself

My father was once in a stake priesthood meeting when the stake president handed out papers and asked each attendee to write their final thoughts as if they knew this would be their last day on earth. Dad wrote, "Please cremate me, place the ashes in a box, and mail them to the Internal Revenue Service accompanied by a note that reads, 'Here you go—now you have it all!'" His comments were, of course, in jest but also reflective of his lifetime struggle to earn a living, pay his taxes, and survive the trials of mortality.

As the result of the fall of Adam and Eve, they, and we as their descendants, received from God this proclamation:

> Cursed shall be the ground for thy sake; in sorrow shalt thou eat of it all the days of thy life.
>
> Thorns also, and thistles shall it bring forth to thee . . . .
>
> By the sweat of thy face shalt thou eat bread, until thou shalt return unto the ground—for thou shalt surely die—for out of it wast thou taken: for dust thou wast, and unto dust shalt thou return. (Moses 4:23–25)

Along with thorns and thistles, we are also subject to pollution, sorrow, taxes, broken bones, disease, trials that test our patience, opposition, betrayal, contention, disappointment (even in marriage), regret, frustration, deceit, weariness, sadness, depression—and so many more afflictions that it can be depressing to even consider them.

Is it of any wonder that, being the mere mortals we are, we often fall short of being the person we would like to be? We sometimes lose our patience and our tongue. We sometimes consciously or inadvertently hurt those we love most. Sometimes we are lazy. Sometimes we get discouraged—particularly when we make comparisons between our inner lives and the public lives of our social-media friends. As time passes, we may lose our exuberance, our energy, and the beauty of our youth.

As we struggle through our mortality with our several human weaknesses, we often find ourselves in a life-place where we do not want to be. Divorce is such a place. Whatever the reasons for or conditions of our divorce, one of the greatest tasks we will ever perform will be to muster up the insight, the meekness, the humility, and the courage to lay our lives on the altar of God's love and allow Him to do for us what we cannot do for ourselves—to heal us of our broken hearts.

If we are to be healed, we will need to properly endure mortality in order to gain eternal life—we must let go of earth in order to grasp heaven. If we have sins to repent of, then repent we must. And if our sin is as subtle as doubting God and His power to heal us, then repent we must. If we are to gain peace and healing, we need to allow God to deal with us as He deals with all. If we are to forgive all, we must forgive ourselves. If we are to overcome blaming others for their weaknesses, then we must overcome blaming ourselves for our own. We must let God suit His mercies to the conditions of all—including ourselves.

STRIVE TO LIVE A "BLAMELESS" LIFE

In the Sermon on the Mount, Jesus taught, "Be ye therefore perfect, even as your Father which is in heaven is perfect" (Matthew 5:48). He does not give us impossible challenges or commands. The hazard we may sometimes encounter is putting ourselves into the role of declaring our own perfection. The key to perfection is to let God guide us along the way and leave judgment and declaration of our perfection to Him in His due time. We focus on the process. He declares the outcome.

The process of attaining eternal, perfect life requires us to master the basic steps along the way—learning to forgive, to have patience, and to not blame God, others, or ourselves. As we work on mastery of these basic principles, we are learning to live a blameless life. Such life is often encouraged through holy writ.

Paul counseled the Corinthian saints the following:

> [Give] no offence in any thing, that the ministry be not blamed:
> But in all things approving ourselves as the ministers of God, in much patience, in afflictions, in necessities, in distresses. (2 Corinthians 6:3–4)

He further charged the Philippian saints,

> Do all things without murmurings and disputings:
> That ye may be blameless and harmless, the sons of God, without rebuke, in the midst of a crooked and perverse nation, among whom ye shine as lights in the world. (Philippians 2:14–15)

Alma, in his great series of soul-searching questions, asks,

> Have ye walked, keeping yourselves blameless before God? Could ye say, if ye were called to die at this time, within yourselves, that ye have been sufficiently humble? That your garments have been cleansed and made white through the blood of Christ, who will come to redeem his people from their sins? (Alma 5:27)

It would be totally ridiculous to assume that any of us reading this book ever had the notion, "I think I will get divorced because I will learn so much through the experience." And yet in a peculiar sort of way, we have the opportunity to learn so much through the experience of divorce. Divorce and all of its attendant heartaches and challenges place us in a crucible of opportunity and growth that is probably not seen as a blessing in the early stages—or perhaps not even in mortality. But through it all, we have a great privilege to learn, by precept and by our own experience, to be blameless—to not blame God, others, nor ourselves—and to learn to live a blameless life.

Note

1. Spencer W. Kimball, *Faith Precedes the Miracle* (Salt Lake City: Deseret Book, 1972), 95–106.

Ten

Correct Doctrine

I HAVE OFTEN SHARED A LITTLE PERSONAL ANECDOTE TO TEACH THE principle of seeking out correct doctrine. When I was a boy, I was blessed to have a horse to ride, and, as I rode around, I kept a good watch on our little town. I particularly enjoyed helping old Frank herd his cows home from the pasture for the night milking. At the appointed hour, I would ride Old Blaze down the country lane and pull up beside Frank. We would then ride along together while herding the cows—which did not require much as the lane was well fenced on both sides.

As we came to the area of a small pond, the cows would stop to drink from Spring Creek, which traversed the gravel lane through a buried steel culvert, with an open area between the culvert's end and the fence. One day, a strange thing happened. As the cows stopped to drink, Frank dismounted his swaybacked, old horse and knelt to drink right with the cows. After a long drink, he raised up, wiped his chin on his sleeve, looked at me, and said, "Young man, I would not trade a drink of this here water for a frosty mug of root beer from Floyd Young's drug store." (To me, it looked about the same.) When I got home, I told Dad of Frank's drink and he asked me a profound question: "Was he upstream or downstream from the cows?" My revulsion lessened as I remembered that Frank was indeed drinking upstream from the cows.

There are many people who are doctrinally drinking downstream from the cows—some dangerously and deliberately, and some perhaps unwittingly. Many fall prey to accepting for truth that which is not true. Particularly during our vulnerable time of divorce, we need to drink pure, upstream waters of truth. The nearer we can come to our Heavenly Father as the pure source of truth, the better guided we will be. Our conduits of truth are such things as promptings from the

Holy Ghost, spoken and written words of our living prophets, and the revealed scriptures. We need to be constantly vetting all we read and hear by asking ourselves such things as: *Is this really the Holy Ghost prompting me? Is this translation of the scripture correct, and am I properly understanding it? Is my imperfect/limited understanding of the scripture consistent with the teachings of our living prophets?*

The dual purpose of this chapter is to teach some basic principles that have helped me in seeking truth and to discuss selected scriptural examples of marriage and divorce that are often misunderstood or misapplied. I hope to help us better understand how we may protect ourselves from the heartache and frustration that comes from misunderstanding.

Eternal Marriage

I have a good friend of many years. We serve and help one another and delight in each other's joys and successes and grieve in each other's heartaches. He is a pastor of a local congregation and has a good, faithful wife. They are blessed with some great children.[1]

Several years ago, my friend shared with me his belief that although he may see his wife and children in the next world, in no way would they be married or joined together as a family. His belief is based, in large measure, on a single Bible verse, "For in the resurrection they neither marry, nor are given in marriage, but are as the angels of God in heaven" (Matthew 22:30). This made me sad for him and his family. I shared with him the "upstream doctrine" of eternal marriage and family, but so far, they are not open to this truth. I pray that someday they will be.

Let us apply some basic principles for finding truth in scripture to this question of marriage in heaven—study it in its proper context, apply the common sense of the truths you already know, seek doctrine from living prophets and modern revelation, and seek the guidance of the Holy Ghost for understanding.

Often we may misunderstand the full meaning of a scriptural passage if we let it "stand alone"—if we do not consider the full background and context of the passage. President Harold B. Lee taught, "With respect to doctrines and meanings of scriptures, let me give you a safe counsel. It is usually not well to use a single passage of scripture [or, I would add, a single sermon] in proof of a point of doctrine unless it is confirmed by modern revelation or by the Book of Mormon. . . . To single out a passage of scripture to prove a point, unless it is [so] confirmed . . . is always a hazardous thing."[2]

Here is the "no marriage" scriptural passage in its broader context:

> The same day came to him the Sadducees, which say that there is no resurrection, and asked him,
>
> Saying, Master, Moses said, If a man die, having no children, his brother shall marry his wife, and raise up seed unto his brother.
>
> Now there were with us seven brethren: and the first, when he had married a wife, deceased, and, having no issue, left his wife unto his brother:
>
> Likewise the second also, and the third, unto the seventh.
>
> And last of all the woman died also.
>
> Therefore in the resurrection whose wife shall she be of the seven? for they all had her.
>
> Jesus answered and said unto them, Ye do err, not knowing the scriptures, nor the power of God.
>
> For in the resurrection they neither marry, nor are given in marriage, but are as the angels of God in heaven. (Matthew 22:23–30)

We may dismiss outright the notion that there is no marriage in heaven. The doctrine of eternal marriage and family has been affirmed by prophets throughout time. President Marion G. Romney taught:

> In each dispensation, from the days of Adam to the days of the Prophet Joseph Smith, the Lord has revealed anew the principles of the gospel. So that while the records of past dispensations, insofar as they are uncorrupted, testify to the truths of the gospel, still each dispensation has had revealed in its day sufficient truth to guide the people of the new dispensation, independent of the records of the past.
>
> I do not wish to discredit in any manner the records we have of the truths revealed by the Lord in past dispensations. What I now desire is to impress upon our minds that the gospel, as revealed to the Prophet Joseph Smith, is complete and is the word direct from heaven to this dispensation. It alone is sufficient to teach us the principles of eternal life. It is the truth revealed, the commandments given in this dispensation through modern prophets by which we are to be governed.[3]

Let us now further consider the context of the question asked of the Savior that prompted His response to the Sadducees. This was an obvious ploy to trap Jesus in His words because the Sadducees actually do not believe in the resurrection anyway—"which say that there is no resurrection" (v. 23).[4] If someone does not believe in the resurrection, then they do not believe in the doctrine of eternal family and eternal life—which I understand to be the type of life enjoyed by our Heavenly Father—as these doctrines are closely tied to and dependent upon perfected, resurrected bodies for those who are to enjoy eternal life. Therefore if we consider the Sadducees in the first verse of our scripture block as the antecedent to the "they" pronoun in the final verse, we are confident that "they" will not be married in heaven, unless they repent of their unbelief and accept and seek the true blessings of eternity.

Now, if we consider the hypothetical seven brothers as the antecedent to the "they" pronoun of the final verse, we may draw the same conclusion, because this scenario is simply a concoction of the unbelieving Sadducees—either way, there is no marriage in heaven for unbelievers who are unwilling to seek out and accept the saving gospel doctrines and make and keep the requisite covenants for eternal life.

Let us now further consider the grand key of modern revelation to help us in our understanding of these often misapplied Bible verses. In a revelation to Joseph Smith, the Lord plainly declared the pure doctrine of eternal marriage. In doing so, He provided very helpful illustrations of three types of marriage: civil marriage, counterfeit "eternal" marriage, and eternal marriage.

Civil Marriage: I know of a couple, now deceased, who were married by civil authority but who had never received the priesthood ordinance of eternal marriage. They truly loved each other and really believed that they would be together forever. My true hope for them is that they have accepted or will yet accept the full gospel and be sealed to each other and to their family forever. But unless they do, they will not be married in heaven. The Lord declared:

> Therefore, if a man marry him a wife in the world, and he marry her not by me nor by my word, and he covenant with her so long as he is in the world and she with him, their covenant and marriage are not of force when they are dead, and when they are out of the world; therefore, they are not bound by any law when they are out of the world.
>
> Therefore, when they are out of the world they neither marry nor are given in marriage. (D&C 132:15–16)

Counterfeit "Eternal" Marriage: A friend told me of the wedding of her nephew, who was married to his bride by a justice of the peace in a civil ceremony. They convinced the judge to add the phrase, "I seal you for time and all eternity" to the ceremony. The Lord has taught:

> And again, verily I say unto you, if a man marry a wife, and make a covenant with her for time and for all eternity, if that covenant is not by me or by my word, which is my law, and is not sealed by the Holy Spirit of promise, through him whom I have anointed and appointed unto this power, then it is not valid neither of force when they are out of the world, because they are not joined by me, saith the Lord, neither by my word; when they are out of the world it cannot be received there, because the angels and the gods are appointed there, by whom they cannot pass; they cannot, therefore, inherit my glory; for my house is a house of order, saith the Lord God. (D&C 132:18)

I have also sometimes called this verse "wannabe eternal marriage"—no matter how sincerely someone may *want to be* married for eternity, unless they marry in the Lord's way, it won't happen. My hope for the young couple I referenced is that they will someday find their way to truth and to the temple and be sealed for time and all eternity by valid priesthood authority. But unless and until they do, there will be no marriage for them in the resurrection.

Eternal Marriage: One of the greatest doctrines of the restored gospel is that of eternal marriages and families. Although God's order and justice do not accommodate marriage beyond mortality except for true sealing by true priesthood authority, His desire for all of His children is that they will marry by true authority for eternity. He has spoken:

> And again, verily I say unto you, if a man marry a wife by my word, which is my law, and by the new and everlasting covenant, and it is sealed unto them by the Holy Spirit of promise, by him who is anointed . . . Ye shall come forth in the first resurrection; and if it be after the first resurrection, in the next resurrection; and shall inherit thrones, kingdoms, principalities, and powers, dominions, all heights and depths . . . it shall be done unto them in all things whatsoever my servant hath put upon them, in time, and through all eternity; and shall be of full force when they are out of the world; and they shall pass by the angels, and the gods, which are set there, to their exaltation

and glory in all things, as hath been sealed upon their heads, which glory shall be a fulness and a continuation of the seeds forever and ever. (D&C 132:19)

So any way we may look at it, there is no marriage in heaven except as the Lord appoints in His own way and by His power and authority. And that way is open to any and all who will humble themselves, accept His truth, make sacred covenants, and endure throughout life in being faithful to those covenants.

Marrying Those Divorced

For those of us who are divorced or divorcing, whether we now or in some future day consider remarriage or whether we don't, I would guess that our lives will likely be impacted in some way large or small by someone's downstream-from-the-cows misunderstanding of this scripture taught by our Savior: "But I say unto you, That whosoever shall put away his wife, saving for the cause of fornication, causeth her to commit adultery: and whosoever shall marry her that is divorced committeth adultery" (Matthew 5:32).

Some may gossip as they offer false assessment to others of your new status. Others may just have misunderstandings of this doctrine that may act as a hindrance to their building a supportive relationship with you. Some may outright cite this passage to you as some kind of warning about any future plans you may have.

I had brief acquaintance with a man who was a widower. He had befriended a lovely divorced lady in his ward. They were of comparable age and interests. He was a scholar of LDS doctrine. One day after I had visited their ward and noticed them sitting together in meeting, I casually asked my friend if they had any intention of marrying. My friend said she had wondered the same thing and knew him well enough that she had asked him. He replied that he would not consider marrying her based on the teaching of the scripture just cited. I was dumbfounded that he would allow such a roadblock to hinder a potential happy and successful path forward. I was also perplexed that in his understanding, he had not gone "upstream" for more pure understanding of this particular verse.

Ten: Correct Doctrine

At the time Jesus gave this counsel on divorce, and to large degree in our day, many had made a mockery out of marriage with little or no consideration of the higher, celestial plan of God-ordained union and fidelity. Many years ago, I heard of a practice of some young people traveling to a city where marriage and divorce requirements were lax, getting married, spending the weekend together, and then getting the marriage annulled before returning home and going their separate ways perhaps only to plan another such weekend with a different partner. Did they really think that a last-minute piece of paper with some fancy words about marriage would absolve their sins and lack of commitment? Jesus's teaching that "whosoever shall marry her that is divorced committeth adultery" certainly had application to their flippant attitude about chastity, marriage, and eternal loyalty. It has a much different application to faithful and committed people who are trying hard to live the gospel and succeed in marriage but, often through no fault nor lack of effort of their own, suffer divorce.

A valuable gem of doctrinal insight and scriptural understanding came to me from a general authority at one of our seminary and institute training meetings years ago. Since it was an informal meeting and since I have adapted his comment to better reflect my personal understanding and style, I will leave him unnamed. Here is the principle: *Current official Church teaching and practice always constitute the correct interpretation of scripture.*[5]

Sometimes people may take a *downstream* approach to understanding a scripture by saying or thinking, "President/Elder So-and-So is speaking contrary to what is said in such-and-such a scripture so therefore he must be wrong." (I am making the assumption here that President/Elder So-and-So is one of our prophets, seers, and revelators speaking by the Spirit in capacity of his official calling.) The *upstream* approach would be more like, "What President/Elder So-and-So is teaching seems contrary to what such-and-such scriptural passage says, so therefore the scripture seems to be in need of correction or clarification."

And I add the caveat that the standard works of the Church are just that—an important "standard" and *check* of the words of our leaders, just as the words of our leaders are a *check* upon the standard works. The key is to examine both and look to the living prophet for clarification of any misunderstandings.

Elder D. Todd Christofferson taught:

> The President of the Church may announce or interpret doctrines based on revelation to him (see, for example, Doctrine and Covenants 138). Doctrinal exposition may also come through the combined council of the First Presidency and Quorum of the Twelve Apostles (see, for example, Official Declaration 2). Council deliberations will often include a weighing of canonized scriptures, the teachings of Church leaders, and past practice. But in the end, just as in the New Testament Church, the objective is not simply consensus among council members but revelation from God. It is a process involving both reason and faith for obtaining the mind and will of the Lord.[6]

Let us consider a *teaching* and a *practice* to help us better understand the Savior's teaching about marriage and divorce.

A Teaching: Elder Dallin H. Oaks taught:

> The kind of marriage required for exaltation—eternal in duration and godlike in quality—does not contemplate divorce. In the temples of the Lord, couples are married for all eternity. But some marriages do not progress toward that ideal. Because 'of the hardness of [our] hearts,' the Lord does not currently enforce the consequences of the celestial standard. He permits divorced persons to marry again without the stain of immorality specified in the higher law. Unless a divorced member has committed serious transgressions, he or she can become eligible for a temple recommend under the same worthiness standards that apply to other members.[7]

A Practice: On Thursday, April 10, 1990, President Howard W. Hunter, as President of the Quorum of the Twelve Apostles, was conducting the regular Thursday meeting of the Twelve in the Salt Lake Temple. After working through the business of the meeting, he asked, "Does anyone have anything that is not on the agenda?" No one responded, so he then made a jaw-dropping announcement, "Well then, if no one else has anything to say, I thought I'd just let you know that I am going to be married this afternoon." After the Brethren recovered somewhat from their amazement, President Hunter went on to say, "Inis Stanton is an old acquaintance from California. I've been visiting with her for some time, and I've decided to be married."[8]

President Hunter had asked President Hinckley to officiate and President Monson and Inis's bishop to serve as witnesses. He informed the rest of the Brethren that no one else was invited. A few days previous, Elder Faust had arranged to have the county clerk come to President Hunter's office to issue the marriage license in an effort to avoid any publicity of the event. "At two o'clock that Thursday afternoon, Howard W. Hunter and Inis Bernice Egan Stanton knelt at the altar in one of the sealing rooms in the temple, and President Hinckley performed the sealing ceremony and pronounced them husband and wife."[9]

So here we had the President of the Quorum of the Twelve who would later become the President of the Church, sealed by a member of the First Presidency in the Salt Lake Temple to Inis Stanton, who had been previously divorced.[10] That is official enough for me—and obviously approved by the Lord, who sanctioned the lives, the marriage, and the service of President and Sister Hunter. *Current official Church teaching and practice always constitute the correct interpretation of scripture.* Matthew 5:32 has been clarified.

As we struggle with the great challenges and trials of divorce, let us not be unduly burdened by confusing and unhealthy misunderstandings, but rather let us drink upstream for pure and correct doctrine, which can provide needed hope and healing.

Notes

1. This is a different pastor friend from the one I referenced earlier at the beginning of chapter two.
2. Clyde J. Williams, ed., *The Teachings of Harold B. Lee* (Salt Lake City: Bookcraft, 1996), 157.
3. Marion G. Romney, "A Glorious Promise," *Ensign*, Jan. 1981, 2.
4. A teacher once shared a little memory hook for me on this matter by telling us that "the Sadducees are *sad, you see*, because they do not believe in the Resurrection."
5. Elder Bruce R. McConkie was not the general authority who shared this thought with us, but I learned from one of my reviewers of this writing of something Elder McConkie did say that seems to confirm my statement. In fact, it is likely that this thought originated with Elder McConkie, who taught, "The proper course of all of us is to stay in the mainstream of the Church. This is the Lord's Church, and it is led by the spirit of inspiration, and the practice of the Church constitutes the interpretation of the scripture"

("Our Relationship with the Lord," [Brigham Young University devotional, Mar. 1982] speeches.byu.edu).
6. D. Todd Christofferson, "The Doctrine of Christ," *Ensign*, May 2012.
7. Dallin H. Oaks, "Divorce," *Ensign*, May 2007, 70.
8. Eleanor Knowles, *Howard W. Hunter* (Salt Lake City: Deseret Book, 1994), 291.
9. Ibid., 292.
10. "Sister Enis Egan Hunter, wife of the late President Howard W. Hunter, dies," *Deseret News,* Oct. 15, 2007.

Eleven

Anxiously Engaged in a Good Cause

A LITTLE OVER FOUR YEARS PREVIOUS TO THE TIME OF THIS WRITING, I had just processed an emergency retirement from my long career in order to help a struggling family. My wife would stay home in Wisconsin to care for our aged aunt who lived with us and to manage our other commitments while I would mostly be living out of state. It was frightening. The day before my departure, my wife arranged an adventure for the two of us and our daughter and her husband. We drove together to the northern forest of our state and received safety training in riding a huge multi-station zip line high above the river and the trees. After our training, we climbed the first of the several huge towers, snapped our harnesses onto the cable and, in turn, stepped off. It was scary.

I went last. I wanted to do this on my own, without anyone there to push me. (Or perhaps I wanted to be able to retreat down the tower alone if I felt I could not go through with it.) After standing paralyzed at the edge of the tower for a few tense moments, I finally stepped out into nothingness. After narrowly escaping a heart attack, I zipped along until I gained footing on the second tower and then prepared to do it all over again. (We had been trained to keep up our momentum or we would not have enough speed for the final slight ascent onto the next platform. If we did not make it, we would need to then do a slow, hand-over-hand pull to gain access to the platform.)

Stepping off the second tower was scary but not quite as bad as the first. Each successive tower was also scary, but my fear markedly diminished as my confidence increased with each tower. We lived, and I was grateful and relieved to climb to the ground from the final tower. The next morning, I said goodbye to my wife, got in my car, and drove away. It was scary, but, due in part to my renewed confidence from my zip line experience, I felt I could somehow succeed.

Divorce could be analogous to this zip line experience—it too is scary, full of uncertainty and new challenges. We will be required to step off several high towers—we may even be pushed out of some of our previous comfort zones—but we have opportunities to learn and grow in ways before unimagined, and we have many people and principles to help us. We will be safe as we follow and apply truth.

I believe that one of the greatest truths to help us heal from divorce and to generally live our lives is taught to us in this scriptural passage:

> Verily I say, men should be anxiously engaged in a good cause, and do many things of their own free will, and bring to pass much righteousness;
>
> For the power is in them, wherein they are agents unto themselves. And inasmuch as men do good they shall in nowise lose their reward. (D&C 58:27–28)

The "good causes" we engage in throughout life are dynamic—ever changing and adjusting throughout our lives. "To every thing there is a season, and a time to every purpose under the heaven" (Ecclesiastes 3:1). Personal healing from divorce is a good cause. This station of life may require more alone time than some others. We need time to ponder and pray and plan our future. And yet life's demands knock at our door, even in the depths of our sorrows, and we must answer. Providing for and sustaining our own life and the lives of others for whom we are responsible are good causes. Working, cleaning, cooking, and washing are noble "good causes" parallel to nurturing, listening, consoling, guiding, and renewing. Of course, we will have to prioritize and choose the better parts of so many things we could do. But always being "anxiously engaged in a good cause" is a major key to our success.

In order to have time for our good causes, we may need to eliminate other causes from our lives that are not so essential or timely. Just yesterday, from the day of this writing, we were out to lunch with friends here in Jerusalem and they told us of a decision they made years ago to mostly eliminate television from their home and how much that decision has blessed their family. Sometimes we may find that we need to eliminate or limit or delay even good, wholesome activities in order to meet the more important demands of the moment. I remember an Apostle once telling of how he had to choose to limit his time on a very rewarding personal hobby in order to meet the demands of his family and his calling.

The grand key we are talking about here is to make sure that we are not wasting our time and our lives. I have long been inspired by President Gordon B. Hinckley's account of a dark, discouraging time during the beginning weeks of his mission when he felt he was not succeeding. I share his experience in his own words:

> I was not well when I arrived. Those first few weeks, because of illness and the opposition which we felt, I was discouraged. I wrote a letter home to my good father and said that I felt I was wasting my time and his money. He was my father and my stake president, and he was a wise and inspired man. He wrote a very short letter to me which said, "Dear Gordon, I have your recent letter. I have only one suggestion: forget yourself and go to work." Earlier that morning in our scripture class my companion and I had read these words of the Lord: "Whosoever will save his life shall lose it; but whosoever shall lose his life for my sake and the gospel's, the same shall save it" (Mark 8:35).
>
> Those words of the Master, followed by my father's letter with his counsel to forget myself and go to work, went into my very being. With my father's letter in hand, I went into our bedroom in the house at 15 Wadham Road, where we lived, and got on my knees and made a pledge with the Lord. I covenanted that I would try to forget myself and lose myself in His service.
>
> That July day in 1933 was my day of decision. A new light came into my life and a new joy into my heart. The fog of England seemed to lift, and I saw the sunlight. I had a rich and wonderful mission experience, for which I shall ever be grateful.[1]

We each need to discover the meaning of "forgetting of self" in our personal situation. It does not mean to forget our own peace or healing. I doubt that President Hinckley neglected his own health and well-being in his renewed effort to focus on others. I am writing with the assumption that we all desire to live happy, productive lives of service and success. We cannot do that if we are not physically or emotionally able to do so.

In a statement that we will discuss further in a later chapter, Elder Neal A. Maxwell offers a vivid key of balancing our lives, "When, for the moment, we ourselves are not being stretched on a particular cross, we ought to be at the foot of someone else's—full of empathy and proffering spiritual refreshment."[2] To me, this statement implies that there are times when our service to others may be more limited as we struggle through our own healing. But it also implies that there is a time when we need to "forget ourselves and go to work." And of course, there are demands and opportunities to help others that are always with us and that we must attend to. And then, as we heal, our capacity to do more increases.

Just less than two years ago from the time of this writing, our son-in-law died in a tragic snowboarding accident, leaving our daughter with three small children, the youngest just four months old. I received the solemn assignment to speak at his funeral. I felt inspired to teach my daughter and those present that I believed that her healing from her grief would come in large measure from her love of and service to her children. I have seen fulfillment of this prophecy as she has done so well, even in times of her greatest sorrows, to nourish, protect, love, and help these sweet angel children as they grow and develop and heal from the loss of their daddy. Our daughter has come far in her healing and has done so with her precious children walking forward with her. As we seek the Spirit, we will know how to serve others while we ourselves heal. The charity that flows from our lives to the blessing of others brings beauty to their lives and to our own.

Within the past few weeks of the time of this writing, my wife and I have traveled with the BYU students on their field trips here in the Holy Land. We have explored from Galilee in the north to the Dead Sea in the south. We have hiked to the headwaters of the Jordan River and witnessed baptisms in the same river downstream from the Sea of Galilee. These experiences, combined with my work on this writing, and particularly of this specific chapter of being anxiously engaged in good causes, have reminded me of a poem I read and was inspired by as a young man. I will share it and then let it stand for you to ponder its meaning in your own life.

ELEVEN: *Anxiously Engaged in a Good Cause*

A very favorite story of mine
Is about two seas in Palestine
One is a sparkling sapphire jewel,
Its waters are clean and clear and cool,
Along its shores children play
And travelers seek it on their way,
And nature gives so lavishly
Her choicest gems to the Galilee.

But to the south the Jordan flows
Into a sea where nothing grows,
No splash of fish, no singing bird,
No children's laughter is ever heard,
The air hangs heavy all around
And nature shuns this barren ground.

Both seas receive the Jordan's flow,
The water is just the same, we know,
But one of the seas, like liquid sun,
Can warm the hearts of everyone,
While farther south another sea
Is dead and dark and miserly.

It takes each drop the Jordan brings
And to each drop it fiercely clings.
It hoards and holds the Jordan's waves
Until like shackled, captured slaves
The fresh, clear Jordan turns to salt
And dies within the Dead Sea's vault.

But the Jordan flows on rapturously
As it enters and leaves the Galilee,
For every drop that the Jordan gives
Becomes a laughing wave that lives
For the Galilee gives back each drop,
Its waters flow and never stop.

And in the laughing, living sea
That takes and gives so generously
We find the way to Life and Living
Is not in Keeping, But in Giving!

Yes, there are two Palestinian seas
And mankind is fashioned after these![3]

Let me briefly share my own personal journey of my attempts to remain actively engaged in good causes as I have been healing from divorce. I do this with the motive of hopefully inspiring some small thought or idea for you to consider as part of your own healing. I have failed in some things and succeeded in others but feel that if I have done anything right it has been to keep moving—to remain anxiously engaged in good causes.

I have mentioned that at the time of my divorce, I felt I had lost most everything I had worked my life for and thought was important. This loss included my profession, which was a major stressor for me, as I had no idea how I would support myself and my family going forward.[4] Gratefully, I was given a period of several months of transition as I was assigned to work in the Human Resources department of the Church, where I was put to work on several different projects. Many blessings came from this assignment—I had a place to go to work each day, and I met many wonderful people who blessed my life. I also learned much about how the Church operates that would benefit my career later on. During this time, I was called to teach the youth of my new ward, which I did not want to do because of my pain and hurt of losing my job doing just such—but I accepted and had a good experience. I was also assigned to home teach some wonderful families who blessed and encouraged me in my forward path.

As my time of transition was coming to an end at the Human Resource department, I realized that I could return to university for one semester and gain a certificate in the field of my master's degree from decades previous that could provide me a career opportunity. I did not want to work this career but enrolled in the semester anyway, which kept my mind busy and introduced me to more great people.

During this semester, my sister introduced me to her friend Carol who had lived in Chicago. She had also been divorced and certainly had empathy for and experience with the healing of broken hearts. We communicated long distance, got together a few times, shared our stories and our desires for life, and then married when I moved to her home in Wisconsin. I considered several career ideas and even tried trading the financial markets by buying and selling stocks in the short term. I failed, but at least I had been blessed to set an "exit limit." The day after I reached it, in my frustration, I announced that I knew one thing I could do, so I dusted off my carpet installation tools, purchased a used van, and introduced myself to some of the big carpet stores in the area. Within a few days, I was fully employed as a carpet installer. I went at it with a vengeance, using it as an outlet for my pent-up frustration.

After about a week, I went into a flooring installation supply business to open an account and purchase supplies. When I gave my name, the older man helping me said, "Oh yes, I have heard of you." I replied, "No, I don't think so. I am new in town." He asked who I was working for and then said, "Yes, that's the place, and I heard there was an old guy there who is carpeting up the town like a crazy man." Yep, that was me—I was definitely anxiously engaged in my installation work.

During the first year of our marriage as I mostly installed carpet, I kept in touch with the administrators of seminary and institute. One day just as I returned home from a job, the phone was ringing. I answered to hear the voice of the administrator of world-wide seminaries and institutes, and he told me, "I just wanted to call you before I go home for the day and tell you that I just came from the Board of Education meeting wherein President Hinckley personally reviewed your file and has approved you for rehire into the Church Educational System (CES)." Oh happy day!

A week later, I was installing carpet at a new home and received a call from the administrator of CES responsible for our area. He congratulated me on my rehire and asked if I would be willing to accept the assignment as coordinator of CES in several stakes of Wisconsin and as director of the institute at UW Madison. I gave a grateful "Yes."

For the next fourteen years, I climbed a steep learning curve in how to coordinate seminaries and institutes and how to train and supervise teachers and work with priesthood leaders in administering the program. I could write a book—not that I would—about the wonderful experiences this work brought to me. During this time, I was blessed with various Church callings and opportunities for service. I became kind of the unofficial "ward handyman" and have been able to do many home repairs and build many things for ward members in need. I began writing books and have published five previous to this one.

Carol and I have served together in teaching early-morning seminary and as Brigham Young University–Idaho Pathway missionaries. We are now gratefully and anxiously engaged as a service couple at the Brigham

Young University Jerusalem Center for Near Eastern Studies. I also serve as the branch president of the Bethlehem Branch and she as the Relief Society president. Through it all, we have together tried to meet the challenges of family and have had many opportunities to render service. We are well along our path of healing from our divorces—and so much of it has come from our efforts to be anxiously engaged in good causes.

In summary, we heal faster as we are actively and anxiously involved in serving. Serving ourselves—or doing what is needed to mend and move our lives forward in our healing process—is a worthy and good cause. Serving others is a major key to our own healing and blesses people in ways we cannot now imagine. As we heal from our own trials, we do well to seek opportunities to help others with theirs.

Life is scary—particularly during the trial of divorce—but if we are willing to overcome our paralysis and step out into the unknown, the Lord will bless us. President Boyd K. Packer taught:

> Shortly after I was called as a General Authority, I went to Elder Harold B. Lee for counsel. He listened very carefully to my problem and suggested that I see President David O. McKay. President McKay counseled me as to the direction I should go. I was very willing to be obedient but saw no way possible for me to do as he counseled me to do.
>
> I returned to Elder Lee and told him that I saw no way to move in the direction I was counseled to go. He said, "The trouble with you is you want to see the end from the beginning." I replied that I would like to see at least a step or two ahead. Then came the lesson of a lifetime: "You must learn to walk to the edge of the light, and then a few steps into the darkness; then the light will appear and show the way before you." Then he quoted these 18 words from the Book of Mormon:
>
> "Dispute not because ye see not, for ye receive no witness until after the trial of your faith" (Ether 12:6).[5]

We must not let our fear of the unknown paralyze our desire to engage in worthy causes. The Lord will guide us and protect us as we heal and as we serve.

Notes

1. Gordon B. Hinckley, "Taking the Gospel to Britain: A Declaration of Vision, Faith, Courage, and Truth," *Ensign*, Jul. 1987.

2. Neal A. Maxwell, *Men and Women of Christ* (Salt Lake City: Bookcraft, 1991), 70.
3. I simply did an internet search to find this poem and in so doing, discovered there are many variations of the story—some in poetry, some written in prose. I liked the one here cited as it seems nearest to my first memory of this poem. This one is credited to Helen Steiner Rice ("The Key to Life and Living," MichaelPPowers.com, accessed March 21, 2018, http://www.michaelppowers.com/prosperity/taking-giving.html).
4. At the time of my hiring to teach seminary, I knew of the policy that a divorced person could not work as a full-time teacher of seminary or institute. I just had no idea that it would ever apply to me.
5. Boyd K. Packer, "The Edge of the Light," *BYU Magazine*, Mar. 1991; as quoted in "Move Forward in Faith," *Ensign*, August 2013.

Twelve

Unto My Holy Mountain

OUR HEAVENLY FATHER'S GREAT PLAN OF HAPPINESS IS A SURE PLAN with an absolute promise of eternal life. Divorce may be a rather annoying bump along the way, but it need not be a roadblock. Nephi portrays Heavenly Father's plan as a gate of "repentance and baptism by water; and then cometh a remission of your sins by fire and by the Holy Ghost (2 Nephi 31:17). He continues: "And then are ye in this strait and narrow path which leads to eternal life" (v. 18). That is pretty much the plan. Once we have accepted it and made our baptismal covenants, we just need to "press forward with a steadfastness in Christ, having a perfect brightness of hope, and a love of God and of all men" (v. 20). As we do so, we then receive the promise, "Wherefore, if ye shall press forward, feasting upon the word of Christ, and endure to the end, behold, thus saith the Father: Ye shall have eternal life" (v. 20). There is nothing mysterious or equivocal about the prospect of eternal life. Heavenly Father means what He says and keeps His promises.

Our journey to eternal life leads us through the temple. Our journey through the temple leads us to eternal life. As we seek out and enter the temple, we are given a great gift or "endowment" from our Heavenly Father. President Brigham Young taught, "Let me give you a definition in brief. Your *endowment* is to receive all those ordinances in the House of the Lord, which are necessary for you, after you have departed this life, to enable you to walk back to the presence of the Father, passing the angels who stand as sentinels . . . and gain your eternal exaltation in spite of earth and hell."[1]

As we have previously discussed and will discuss further, we all must change—we must repent of the ways of the world and grasp the principles of heaven if we are to have eternal life. To help us do so,

Heavenly Father has provided temples throughout the earth. President Boyd K. Packer taught, "It has been my observation that the temple transforms the individual and makes abundantly worthwhile any efforts made to get there."[2]

In the previous chapter, we discussed the need to be engaged in good things, which entails taking risks and being willing to step out into the darkness. As we do so, the Lord leads us along. One of the greatest blessings of my life came from my new appointment to coordinate seminaries and institutes in Wisconsin and Upper Michigan. One of the sweetest experiences of that assignment was the fellowship I had with my fellow coordinators scattered across ten Midwestern states. We met together several times each year for a few days of training and camaraderie. They became some of my dearest friends.

One day I received a phone call from one of these colleagues who was a member of the training council, responsible for organizing our group meetings. He informed me that the council had discussed their desires for the coming year and that they wanted me to teach three 90-minute sessions on the topic of *What Isaiah Teaches Us about the Temple*. This was, for me, definitely one of those "be willing to step off the high tower" experiences. I barely knew what Isaiah was talking about. I responded only half-jokingly to my friend, "Wow, I did not know Isaiah taught about the temple." Of course, I knew there were temple references in his teachings, like "the mountain of the Lord's house shall be established in the top of the mountains" (Isaiah 2:2), but I had no idea of the depth and multitude of his temple imagery and teachings until I engaged in my study.

I had a great year in preparing for and giving my three presentations, which in turn led me to teaching some special Isaiah-specific classes at the Institute and also my eventual writing of and publishing a book on the topic.[3] I had no idea at the outset of my Isaiah journey that I would find teachings so profound and far-reaching as that of the example of the eunuch in chapter 56 and the application we may draw to all people—particularly those of us who are divorced—from the Lord's counsel and promise of temple blessings to someone so seemingly out of reach of the desired blessings of eternal life.

In the beginning verses of this chapter, Isaiah reviews the charge and the promises of following the gospel path, "Blessed is the man that doeth this, and the son of man that layeth hold on it; that keepeth the sabbath from polluting it, and keepeth his hand from doing any evil" (Isaiah 56:2). He then anticipates the self-doubt that some may have, "neither let the eunuch say, Behold, I am a dry tree" (v. 3). (A eunuch has no ability of procreation and is part of a "class of emasculated men attached to the courts of eastern rulers. They were employed to watch over the harems and also were often given positions as trusted officials."[4] Often their condition was effected upon them at an early age and against their will).

As I have pondered the plight of the poor eunuch, for me he has become somewhat of a representative poster child for all of us who are sometimes made to feel as outcasts from the Lord's plan. Imagine the eunuch, who has little prospect of marriage and no prospect of posterity in his mortal lifetime, transposed into one of our modern congregations where we regularly sing about families being together for eternity and teach of the importance of strong marriages and families. What is he to do? Why should he make an effort to set his course upon the gospel path to eternal life?

And as I have further pondered the plight of the eunuch, I have realized that he would not be the only one in our congregations perhaps feeling hopeless at the prospect of eternal life. What about the woman or man who has always desired and sought eternal marriage but has no prospect of such? What about the married couple who would like to bear children but are not able to do so? What about the young man whose mental illness blocks his path to a happy family life? What about the man or woman whose same-gender attraction precludes a happy, childbearing marriage? And what about those of us who were blessed with spouse and children and even sealed in the temple and must then endure the pain and suffering of having it all seemingly unravel in the court of divorce? Where is our hope?

Let us find out. The Lord says, "Neither let the son of the stranger, that hath joined himself to the Lord, speak, saying, The Lord hath utterly separated me from his people: neither let the eunuch say, Behold, I am a dry tree" (v. 3). We must think larger than mortality, because obviously the eunuch is a dry tree (no posterity) here, but the Lord apparently has a greater plan and purpose beyond mortality and admonishes him to think in a broader spectrum. Even though we are divorced and possibly thinking our eternal sealing is broken, we need to hold on and seek further enlightenment.

The Lord then repeats His charge before explaining the blessings, thus emphasizing His apparent necessary conditions for redemption from our broken mortality and qualification for what He has in store for us, "For thus saith the Lord unto the eunuchs that keep my sabbaths, and choose the things that please me, and take hold of my covenant" (v. 4). Let us consider this charge with a brief comment about each:

Keep My Sabbaths: I believe that sincere, heartfelt, personal worship in keeping the Sabbath is a benchmark activity—an indicator of our gospel commitment across the board. I am pleased with the efforts made by our Church leaders to help us elevate our keeping of the Sabbath by intimately engaging in worship through music, spoken word, repentance, service, personal study, personal pondering, and recommitment to gospel principles.

Choose the Things That Please Me: If we were to choose to lie, steal, commit adultery, dishonor our parents, or anything else of evil nature, our Lord would be displeased. We "choose the things that please" Him by keeping His commandments—by *doing* the things He knows will bring us and others the greatest peace and happiness and that will chart our path firmly to eternal life.

Take Hold of My Covenant: Covenants we make with God are not in the realm of negotiated deals wherein we lobby for what we think is best for us. To "take hold of [God's] covenant" is to demonstrate the faith and humility to trust in Him and in His wisdom and plan for us, and then joyfully and obediently accept the offering He gives us. He, in His omniscience, sets the terms of the covenants. We accept His offering through making and keeping of our baptismal and temple covenants, and then by always remembering and renewing them by our sincere worship throughout the duration of our lives.

And now the Lord pronounces the great blessing to all who will accept and keep covenants:

> Even unto them will I give in mine house and within my walls a place and a name better than of sons and of daughters: I will give them an everlasting name, that shall not be cut off.
>
> Also the sons of the stranger, that join themselves to the Lord, to serve him, and to love the name of the Lord, to be his servants, every

one that keepeth the sabbath from polluting it, and taketh hold of my covenant;

    Even them will I bring to my holy mountain, and make them joyful in my house of prayer: their burnt offerings and their sacrifices shall be accepted upon mine altar; for mine house shall be called an house of prayer for all people. (vs. 5–7)

The phrases, "mine house" and "my holy mountain" are phrases of temple imagery. No matter our life or marital status, physical or emotional impairment, or whatever other roadblock to eternal life we may perceive—if we will humble ourselves and chart our forward course to the temple, the Lord will give us "better than of sons and of daughters." I have marveled about what could be better than sons and daughters, because we are taught that forever families are to be our greatest joy. Not only is that our teaching, it is my personal experience of greatest joy with my wife, my sons, and my daughter and grandchildren. And then I think again of the eunuch—the fulfillment of the promise of sons and daughters for him will have to be in a future world well beyond the tears, trials, pollutions, addictions, and heartaches of this world. As I imagine life with my family in such an exalted and pure condition, I understand. Even better than the joy I have from my loved ones here will be the continued joy I will have with them in the celestial and pure world beyond the grave. I get it and I love it!

There is no greater blessing than to be eternally "joyful" with our Heavenly parents and with our eternal families. The knowledge that our extended families and our friends have the same potential and promise of living joyfully with Heavenly Father and an eternal family is a sweet prospect, even though they—and we—may be "eunuchs" here on earth. We gain such promise by charting a true course to the Lord's holy temple.

Wherever you are in your journey, I pray that you may seek the blessings of the temple. I assure that it will be a major step in healing your broken heart. If you have not ever been to the temple or have not been for a long time, I plead with you to go. You can begin today by requesting a temple recommend interview with your bishop. Whether your recommend would be granted now or after a time of preparation is of no matter—what matters is that you are facing the right direction and seeking with faith to go to the "holy mountain"—the Lord's house.[5]

Notes

1. Brigham Young, comp. John A. Widtsoe, *Discourses of Brigham Young* (Salt Lake City: Deseret Book, 1971), 637.
2. Boyd K. Packer, *The Holy Temple* (Salt Lake City: Bookcraft, 1980), 21.
3. Reg Christensen, *Unlocking Isaiah: Lessons and Insights That Draw Us to the Savior* (American Fork Utah: Covenant Communications, Inc., 2013).
4. Bible Dictionary, s.v., "eunuch."
5. When I served as bishop, I got a call from a man whose wife was literally on her deathbed. She wanted her temple recommend renewed. I thought, *Why? She won't be using it.* But I called the counselor in the stake presidency and we went and visited her and gave her a renewed recommend. She died a few weeks later. I made a self-promise at that time that I would do the same—never let my temple recommend expire in my mortality. I highly recommend the same course for one and all.

Thirteen

More Intelligent than They All

Let me introduce you to my three pesky friends whom I have been trying to unfriend for years, but they keep coming around. I sincerely do not like them and I know that my relationship with them is not a healthy one—they only want to destroy my peace and confidence. Their names are *Shoulda, Coulda,* and *Woulda*.[1]

I believe that one of the great hazards of our lives—and particularly during the more vulnerable time of divorce—is listening to these three unwelcome pests. They try to distract us by constantly reminding us what we *should have* done, or *could have* done, or *would have* done to have prevented the dissolution of our marriage. They continually try to drag us into the pit of comparative thinking in order to discourage us in our efforts to go forward and create a new, elevated life. (But I must concede that sometimes they speak truths important for us to learn—I just do not believe they are the best of counselors in their continuous harangue. We have higher, truer, and more trusted sources of positive motivation and inspiration.)

Within days of my divorce, a friend and former colleague (supervisor, actually) called me to come and help him with a home repair. As we accomplished the task, he gave me good counsel and much encouragement. The most memorable thing he taught me was that, as much as I may wish otherwise, I could not turn back time. What had happened had happened, and I needed to now go forward. About this time, my bishop, who had replaced me as bishop, offered me the same advice: "Your problem is that you have stayed too long and tried too hard—now get on with your life and go forward in seeking peace and happiness."

Perhaps you are struggling with comparative thinking and beating yourself up with regrets of what you could have or should have or would have done differently. I think we all do to one degree or another. "If I had just married someone like him/her, we would not have had these problems," or, "I should have done such and such," or, "My family could never be the celestial family that they are," or, "I could never measure up to her/his spiritual stature," or, "They don't know the meaning of trial and heartache," or, "He/she is so lucky. I wonder why God seems to be picking on me," or, "I bet they are not as happy as they pretend to be." And so go the comparisons—if we allow them. Everyone has trials—we just need to get beyond them.

I was once on the high council and had a speaking assignment in my own ward. Before the meeting began, I was looking at the people individually and thinking, "We are such a great ward of good saints. There are just not many problems here." About a year later, I was called as bishop and a year or so after that I sat on the stand awaiting the start of the meeting. I recalled then the day of my assessment of the people from a few years previous and looked over all of the families in the ward once again. This time my reaction was, "We do not have a single family in the ward who is not struggling with serious challenges of one type or another." Sometimes people struggle with well publicized trials; other times, the battles are silent and hidden deep in the heart.

The truth is that we really do not know the full extent of another person's trial, success, heartache, joy, sorrow, or capacity to face opposition. And even if we did, we cannot compare it to our own and draw any substantive conclusions. What we should have done in the past is mostly irrelevant at this point—except to process enough memory of events to effect positive future change. The past is to learn from, not to live in. The degree of another person's good or ill or success or failure does not determine our own status. Our Heavenly Father deals with us one by one and judges us individually by how we follow His counsel and how we treat others.

Divorce is a great pivot point in our lives. Our gift of agency is put to the test more at this juncture than perhaps at any other time of our mortality. We are left to decide where we want to go and who we want to follow to get there.

On the Mormon pioneer trail, approximately halfway between Winter Quarters and Salt Lake City, Chimney Rock dominates the view of the vast plain. This magnificent approximately 300-foot-tall rock "chimney" rises above the prairie floor and rests atop a 200-foot-high rounded base.[2] This inspiring landmark could be seen for days by the weary Saints who would often stop there to mend, cook, and rest in the cool shadow of the rock. Many carved their names in the rock as a memorial to their passage.

One valiant sister did not quite make this milestone. Mary Murray Murdoch joined the Church in Scotland in 1851 at age sixty-seven after her husband was killed in a mining accident. She was a small woman of four feet seven inches and weighed about ninety pounds, thus earning her nickname Wee Granny. John, one of her eight children, and his family left Scotland in 1852 and made the difficult journey to the Salt Lake Valley, where they saved enough money to bring Wee Granny to them. She sailed from Liverpool, England, to New York, rode a train to the Midwest, and joined the Martin Handcart Company at Iowa City. The difficult journey through the harsh prairie weakened Wee Granny to the point of exhaustion. On October 2, 1856, she died about ten miles east of Chimney Rock. Her tender, dying words are engraved on her memorial stone marker near the Chimney Rock visitors' center *"Tell John I died with my face toward Zion."*[3]

To die with one's face toward Zion is to die with the hope of a glorious resurrection and of eternal life. I realized years ago that the third chapter of Abraham is an inspiring treatise on dealing with our comparative thinking and seeking eternal life.

Abraham tells of his great vision wherein the Lord showed him the stars and planets of the heavens and taught him of their creation. He describes a fascinating vision of the creation of planets in various spheres and time frames. Some have used this account to declare that our earth was created in six thousand years because of the phrase from the scripture, "that one revolution was a day unto the Lord, after his manner of reckoning, it being one thousand years according to the time appointed unto that whereon thou standest" (Abraham 3:4).

This theory does not work for me because we are not told if our earth, where we assume Abraham was standing at the time of his vision, was kept in its same orbit and time ratio through the entire process and if, upon finalization of the creation, it remained in the same spot. I have wondered that when God creates worlds if perhaps He moves them around from place to place until they are positioned into their intended location—akin to how I construct a cedar chest and sometimes move it around and even let it stand idle for a time for glue joints or finish to cure. We simply do not know all of the details of the creation.

Abraham's marvelous vision helps me process and solidify what I do know—that God is a "great big" God. The late Carl Sagan said:

> In some respects, science has far surpassed religion in delivering awe. How is it that hardly any major religion has looked at science and concluded, 'This is better than we thought!' The Universe is much bigger than our prophets said—grander, more subtle, more elegant. God must be even greater than we dreamed?' Instead, they say, 'No, no, no! My god is a little god and I want him to stay that way.' A religion, old or new, that stressed the magnificence of the Universe as revealed by modern science might be able to draw forth reserves of reverence and awe hardly tapped by the conventional faiths. Sooner or later, such a religion will emerge."[4]

I believe in a great big God who has the capacity and the vision not only to create and manage worlds without number but also to help us with our personal and individual heartaches. He does not give up on us just because we may stumble and fall and do something we *shoulda* and *coulda* done differently—and maybe *woulda* done if we weren't fighting this fierce battle of our breaking hearts. In His eternal time zone, He has the time to be patient with us as we mourn and heal and learn and grow. He lives in a realm "where all things for their glory are manifest, past, present, and future, and are continually before the Lord" (D&C 130:7). He has time, patience, and wisdom to nurture, tutor, and love us with His divine and perfect love.

Abraham describes comparisons of stars and planets, designating one as closest to His throne:

> And thus there shall be the reckoning of the time of one planet above another, until thou come nigh unto Kolob, which Kolob is after the reckoning of the Lord's time; which Kolob is set nigh unto the throne of God, to govern all those planets which belong to the same order as that upon which thou standest. (Abraham 3:9)

Abraham then shares a sweet, intimate view of the Lord:

> Thus I, Abraham, talked with the Lord, face to face, as one man talketh with another; and he told me of the works which his hands had made;
> And he said unto me: My son, my son (and his hand was stretched out), behold I will show you all these. And he put his hand upon mine eyes, and I saw those things which his hands had made, which were many; and they multiplied before mine eyes, and I could not see the end thereof. (vs. 11–12)

I love this passage because our Heavenly Father and our Savior know us personally as sons and daughters and, just as They reach out and touch Abraham, They have the capacity to reach out and touch us in our times of joy and of sorrow. They do not abandon nor do They forget us, even though They may not always be before our eyes as we are before Theirs.

The Lord reveals to Abraham some true comparative thinking on a grand and never-ending scale as He shares a description of His creations:

> If two things exist, and there be one above the other, there shall be greater things above them; therefore Kolob is the greatest of all the Kokaubeam that thou hast seen, because it is nearest unto me. (v. 16)

The Lord now zeros in on His purpose of teaching Abraham, and us, these truths:

> Now, if there be two things, one above the other, and the moon be above the earth, then it may be that a planet or a star may exist above it; and there is nothing that the Lord thy God shall take in his heart to do but what he will do it. (v. 17)

What is it that the Lord has taken into His heart to do with His children? My thoughts go directly to His "mission statement" as revealed to Moses, "For behold, this is my work and my glory—to bring to pass the immortality and eternal life of man" (Moses 1:39). He is determined to bless us to the full extent of our willingness to accept of His offering!

Abraham's vision now makes a profound shift from a discussion of stars and planets to that of eternal souls:

> Howbeit that he made the greater star; as, also, if there be two spirits, and one shall be more intelligent than the other . . .

> These two facts do exist, that there are two spirits, one being more intelligent than the other; there shall be another more intelligent than they. (vs. 18–19)

If we choose to unjustly compare ourselves with others, we lose. We will always fall short because there will always be an upward spiral of more intelligent beings—all the way to the throne of God. We do not have to look far to see someone smarter, or richer, or more friendly, or more adept at sociality, or better at singing or football or dancing or whatever character trait or achievement we wish to plug in here. If our goal is to be the very best at performance, we are disappointed. If our goal is to become more spiritual than others, we are misguided in our wish and defeated by our very attitude before we even begin. In God's realm and purpose, He would desire that *all* of His children gain eternal life.

In my opinion and pondering, the Lord now nails the malady of comparative thinking and offers the antidote for it. He plainly and simply declares what I believe to be the bottom line of the comparative thinking discussion:

> I am the Lord thy God, I am more intelligent than they all. (v. 19)

If any being *except* God were to make such a statement, we would discount it as idle, hyperbolic arrogance, akin to what we might hear in a political campaign. But this is our Savior speaking and He is speaking simple and pure fact—and not that He is just more intelligent than *any* mortal soul, but that he is more intelligent than the combined knowledge of *all* mortal souls. And He speaks in total humility and desire to help and succor each and every one of us through our trials.

God does not reveal to us that portion of His intelligence about the age of the earth or the details of how He created it—He leaves such trivia to our own entertainment and study. What He does reveal is the "why" of the creation of the earth and of His nature and His capacity to save us. Abraham continues describing the Lord's grandeur:

> Wherein my wisdom excelleth them all, for I rule in the heavens above, and in the earth beneath, in all wisdom and prudence, over all the intelligences thine eyes have seen from the beginning. . . . We will go down, for there is space there, and we will take of these materials, and we will make an earth whereon these may dwell;

And we will prove them herewith, to see if they will do all things whatsoever the Lord their God shall command them;

And they who keep their first estate shall be added upon; and they who keep not their first estate shall not have glory in the same kingdom with those who keep their first estate; and they who keep their second estate shall have glory added upon their heads for ever and ever. (vs. 21, 24–26 [21–26])

I have sometimes wondered how God, if He were a sports fan, would react to our mortal competitions. I have imagined that He is likely not so impressed with the awarding of the Super Bowl trophy, something won by engaging in major comparative thinking, as He would be with two athletes running a Special Olympics race, perhaps helping each other as each stumbles and falls, crossing the finish line arm in arm together.

I have often taught my students that it is not nearly as important where we are on our progressive path to eternal life as it is which direction we are facing and with how much diligence we are moving in the right direction. Wee Granny knew this. Our fallen world will distract us and try to get us to face the wrong direction. Life can get a bit confusing in a world that puts only the best on stage or through to the playoffs. Yes, we all may be improved and inspired by the performance—we do not disparage sincere display of public talents—we simply need to remember that all have talents and that most of the important work of the world is done off the field and off the stage. The work of salvation is a quiet process effected mostly in the hearts of individual souls.

The *shoulda, coulda, wouldas* of our lives are irrelevant except to learn from—they are ancient history, even if they happened just yesterday. Our comparative thinking may have purpose if we learn how to *truly* rejoice in another's success and let it inspire our own, without allowing it to discourage or misguide our personal spiritual development. Elder Neal A. Maxwell taught, "Our only valid spiritual competition is with our old selves, not with each other."[5]

Our God is a "great big" God who has the intelligence, the power, and the desire to lead us back to Him. He will not forget us and will not give up on us, even when we may feel like giving up on ourselves. If we are willing to plant our feet on the gospel path, He will walk by us and lead us along. As we prove ourselves by living as He would have us live, we will discover why He is "more intelligent than they all"—it is so He can nurture us and save us and mend our broken hearts.

Notes

1. I honestly did not know until I did an internet search the very day of this writing that a popular performer had memorialized these three characters in song. I have thought for years that I had christened them. Oh well!
2. From Nebraska's government website: https://history.nebraska.gov/rock.
3. Anne R. McDonald and Gaylen Young, "Descendants Honor Faithful 'Wee Granny,'" *Church News of the Church of Jesus Christ of Latter-day Saints*, July 28, 2001.
4. Carl Sagan, *Pale Blue Dot: A Vision of the Human Future in Space* (New York: Random House, 1994), 50.
5. Neal A. Maxwell, *Not My Will, But Thine* (Salt Lake City: Deseret Book, 2002), 70.

Fourteen

Hope for the Children

In my conversations with divorced or divorcing people, I have heard repetitions, in one form or another, of a discussion with their former spouse that went something like this: "But what about the children? How will they fare?" Reply: "They will be just fine."

Wrong! They will not be just fine. How could anyone expect them to be just fine when their whole world seems to have been torn apart? Well, ultimately they will be fine, but their hearts will ache just as yours does—they will need to heal just as you do. They will each suffer at some level—some perhaps more in silence and others in very public and outspoken ways. They may act in ways you do not recognize or expect. They may turn away from you. They may cling to you. They may do things that are hurtful to themselves or others. They may feel guilty, as if they somehow caused the divorce. They may feel embarrassed. They may feel like they have to choose sides in your divorce battle. They may fear their future potential for successful marriage and family. They may try to sabotage your new relationships. They may experience a crisis of faith—particularly if your marriage was sealed in the holy temple. They may have mixed and varied emotions hour to hour and day to day. They need your love, counsel, empathy, charity, forgiveness, patience, time, and space—and perhaps professional help.

As parents, you will hurt for them. You may experience feelings of total helplessness in regard to how to comfort and nurture them. Your own guilt may be accentuated as you fall short of being the kind of parent you wished you could be. Yet you will feel success as you connect and see their healing and progress. Your healing will be accelerated by theirs. As you move closer to the Lord and His saving grace and feel the healing peace that He brings to you, you will better realize the needs of your children. The more you can help them see what you see and feel in your healing, the less painful and more peaceful their journey will be. They will face many, if not most of, the challenges you do in one way or another, and you and they will discover that all of the principles needed for your well-being are also needed for theirs.

In this chapter, I will try to accomplish two objectives: to offer practical tips for helping our children in minimizing their suffering, and to remind us of the hope and vision that we need in order to keep our focus on our eternal perspective and keep us moving in the right direction.

Faithful Actions

"Faithful Actions" are actions we as parents can take, while exercising our faith, to help our children navigate this rough road—to help minimize their suffering and help them to "be just fine"—hopefully sooner than later. I have reached out to some of my friends who have been divorced for help on this section, and they have graciously responded. I share their comments anonymously and intermingle some of my own thoughts among theirs. You may find some of the statements to be contradictory to some of the others—I will leave you to sort out what may be most helpful for you and your family.

- "Seminary, Primary, Young Men, and Young Women organizations are all supporting programs of the Church that can help children through the divorce process. Visit with leaders and let them know of the specific challenges your child may be facing. This will better help engage them as members of your support team."
- "'Our home is not broken! We are not a broken family!' We repeated this any time the issue came up, like stated in some talks at Church. Heavenly Father was my companion in raising my children."
- "Family home evening was a great necessity for us. I bore my testimony regularly to my children in FHE. We planned for when the boys would serve missions. We discussed the value of education to create a clear vision with each child of what their future would look like."

- "My house was not always clean, but my kids knew they were loved."
- "My wife may have expressed her hurts and frustrations to me but she never did to her children. She never dissed her former spouse in front of the children. I tried to be understanding and helpful."
- "It is important that we include our children, of any age, in our temple experiences. Placing their names on the prayer roll can result in miraculous blessings. (And it is fine to place our own names there as well.) Teach them that—even though our marriage failed—when they go to the temple to be married, we will be there with them."
- "Live the principles of the gospel. Stay true to the covenants and commitments you have made. No matter what I suffered, I made sure that I was in church every Sunday and that I was doing my best for the children."
- "I never gave up on my children. I sought for every opportunity to love them and serve them."
- "There is no 'one-size-fits-all' counsel for parents and children going through divorce as we all are unique. We ride the waves of grief at different rhythms depending on our age, the stress we feel, the support we have, and the closeness of the Spirit in our lives."
- "I set up daily work schedules for the children where we all worked together on a list of chores that were usually needed but in some cases were only designed to keep us doing something together. I also tried to make the projects hard enough that when we were done we would be glad to get in the house and go to sleep."
- "This may sound weird, but family home evening just did not work for us. When I have mentioned to my adult children that I feel I failed at FHE, they have told me that what I did do was to weave the gospel through every aspect of our lives—by living it."
- "I tried to find times to be with my children and to talk to them. When I could not, I wrote them long, personal letters of encouragement."
- "The one-parent buy-off—where one parent seeks to buy the child's affection, loyalty, and allegiance by giving them things, often upon request of the child—may be one of the most devastating problems associated with divorce. When you are 16, it is hard to see past a shiny new car."

Fourteen: Hope for the Children

- "I did not have a stream of potential daddies coming through the door. My children were my absolute priority. I did not worry about finding a husband—there was so much healing and growing that needed to take place. And my babies needed ME."
- "If at all possible, let mom be at home with the children."
- "I attended all of the children's events that I could—generally all of the home events and occasionally the away events."
- "I counseled with my bishop and other leaders about how they could help bless my children."
- "Help your children understand that, even though your sealing to your spouse has been compromised, they are still sealed up unto eternal life. Help them to not be overly concerned about this matter but teach them to live their personal lives worthy of eternal life and to trust the Lord, who will make all things right in His due time."
- "I have tried to be an example of living the gospel. I have kept my covenants and regularly attended the temple."
- "My wife has always listened to the children as they have vented their frustrations for the actions of their father. This she has done in an understanding manner, helping them to understand that despite his failings, they still need to love him and remember that he is their father."
- "The only thing worth fighting for in divorce is the custody and well-being of the children, and that seems to be pretty well established in most cases by the courts, so once that is agreed upon, in my opinion, there is nothing else worth fighting for."
- "I needed to determine the negotiable and the nonnegotiable so I could let go of those things that did not matter. For example, I simply did not worry about beds being made every day. Some battles just were not worth it. I saved my time and energy for the important stuff."
- "My new wife and I set ground rules for our home to follow the prophet, read the scriptures, and support the children in Church assignments, scouts, school functions, sports, music, theater, or whatever they were involved in."
- "My children saw me on my knees by my bed every day as they passed my room. As adults, they have mentioned how much of an example this was for them."

- "We made a commitment that there would be no 'stepchildren.' We treated hers and mine equally. The result is that I love all of our children and never think of them differently than my own."
- "I told my children that they could never use coming from a single-parent home as an excuse for anything."
- "Realize that our children may differ from us in their view of events. As siblings, they may disagree. There is no point in us going to extremes to set the record straight—in the end, truth will prevail."
- "My wife helped her children understand that despite her former husband's moral transgressions, Heavenly Father still loved him and wanted him to repent and come back."
- "Love all of your children equally and support them as such."

I am grateful for the goodness of these friends who have shared their wisdom with us. Their children are blessed to have such good and devoted parents who understand the principles of eternity and who have so valiantly applied these principles to the lives of their children as they suffered together through the trial of divorce. And if you could only know their children as I have been privileged to know some of them, you would know that they are just fine, after all. For that, I am also very grateful.

Doctrines of Redemption

I will deliberately not share many of my own words in this section, but rather will cite some profound words of hope and counsel from our leaders for you to ponder and process. What I do share is an ongoing theme of this book and of my personal belief that we and our children will be fine as we follow our Savior and keep our gospel covenants. I want to give particular hope and encouragement to those of us who, despite our sincere efforts and desire, have suffered the pain of having our children wander strange paths.

I want to first clarify a passage of scripture that is sometimes misunderstood, "And again, inasmuch as parents have children in Zion, or in any of her stakes which are organized, that teach them not to understand the doctrine of repentance, faith in Christ the Son of the living God, and of baptism and the gift of the Holy Ghost by the laying on of the hands, when eight years old, the sin be upon the heads of the parents" (D&C 68:25).

Note that the word "sin" in the last line is singular and, I believe, has as its antecedent the phrase "that teach them not" earlier in the verse. Yes, we are responsible for the teaching of the basic gospel to our children, and if we do not teach them, then we are guilty of not teaching them; but we are not responsible for their individual sins if they do not accept and follow what we teach. Remember the truth stated in the articles of our faith, "We believe that men will be punished for their own sins, and not for Adam's transgression" (Article of Faith 1:2). And I think we could safely add the phrase, "nor for the sins of their parents, nor for the sins of their children."

At a challenging time when one of my own children was wandering a dangerous path, I sought counsel from my bishop. I prayed, counseled, loved, went to the temple, and sought revelation, and yet nothing seemed to be changing. My bishop had spiritually prepared for our session and, in our meeting, gave me much counsel. He also gave me an inspired priesthood blessing of hope and encouragement and shared with me a quotation from an Apostle that he had felt inspired to share. It has been a treasured gem ever since. Elder Richard G. Scott said:

> If you are free of serious sin yourself, don't suffer needlessly the consequence of another's sins. As a wife, husband, parent, or loved one, you can feel compassion for one who is in the gall of bitterness from sin. Yet you should not take upon yourself a feeling of responsibility for those acts. When you have done what is reasonable to help one you love, lay the burden at the feet of the Savior. He has invited you to do that so that you can be free from pointless worry and depression. As you so act, not only will you find peace but will demonstrate your faith in the power of the Savior to lift the burden of sin from a loved one through his repentance and obedience.[1]

I was once listening to President Boyd K. Packer speak of saving truths applied to the lives of our wandering children. He said some impressive and inspiring things and quoted a sublime statement from the Prophet Joseph Smith (see associated reference below). His words and the words of Joseph Smith were very comforting to me. Some months later, I was pleased to open the *Ensign* magazine and find this quote from Joseph Smith, along with some other great messages, shared as "stand-alone" passages on a single page.[2]

In conclusion of this chapter, I will take basically the same approach—I will share the quotations and let them stand alone for your perusal and pondering. But I will add a footnoted reference to a great article that you may choose to read that further explores the topics herein and clarifies some potential misunderstandings, such as a wrong concept of unconditional salvation for those who disobey God's commandments.[3]

Of Joseph Smith, Orson F. Whitney said:

> The Prophet Joseph Smith declared—and he never taught a more comforting doctrine—that the eternal sealings of faithful parents and the divine promises made to them for valiant service in the Cause of Truth, would save not only themselves, but likewise their posterity. Though some of the sheep may wander, the eye of the Shepherd is upon them, and sooner or later they will feel the tentacles of Divine Providence reaching out after them and drawing them back to the fold. Either in this life or the life to come, they will return. They will have to pay their debt to justice; they will suffer for their sins; and may tread a thorny path; but if it leads them at last, like the penitent Prodigal, to a loving and forgiving father's heart and home, the painful experience will not have been in vain. Pray for your careless and disobedient children; hold on to them with your faith. Hope on, trust on, till you see the salvation of God.[4]

President Brigham Young said:

> Let the father and mother, who are members of this Church and Kingdom, take a righteous course, and strive with all their might never to do a wrong, but to do good all their lives; if they have one child or one hundred children, if they conduct themselves towards them as they should, binding them to the Lord by their faith and prayers, I care not where those children go, they are bound up to their parents by an everlasting tie, and no power of earth or hell can separate them from their parents in eternity; they will return again to the fountain from whence they sprang.[5]

President Lorenzo Snow declared:

> If you succeed in passing through these trials and afflictions and receive a resurrection you will, by the power of the Priesthood, work and labor,

as the Son of God has, until you get all your sons and daughters in the path of exaltation and glory. This is just as sure as that the sun rose this morning over yonder mountains. Therefore, mourn not because all your sons and daughters do not follow in the path that you have marked out to them, or give heed to your counsels. Inasmuch as we succeed in securing eternal glory, and stand as saviors, and as kings and priests to our God, we will save our posterity.[6]

President Boyd K. Packer taught:

The measure of our success as parents . . . will not rest solely on how our children turn out. That judgment would be just only if we could raise our families in a perfectly moral environment, and that now is not possible.

It is not uncommon for responsible parents to lose one of their children, for a time, to influences over which they have no control. They agonize over rebellious sons or daughters. They are puzzled over why they are so helpless when they have tried so hard to do what they should.

It is my conviction that those wicked influences one day will be overruled. . . .

We cannot overemphasize the value of temple marriage, the binding ties of the sealing ordinance, and the standards of worthiness required of them. When parents keep the covenants they have made at the altar of the temple, their children will be forever bound to them.[7]

Notes

1. Richard G. Scott, "To Be Free of Heavy Burdens," *Ensign*, Nov. 2002.
2. "Hope for Parents of Wayward Children," *Ensign*, Sept. 2002.
3. See David A. Bednar, "Faithful Parents and Wayward Children: Sustaining Hope While Overcoming Misunderstandings," *Ensign*, March 2014.
4. Orson F. Whitney, in Conference Report, Apr. 1929, 110.
5. Brigham Young, as quoted in Joseph Fielding Smith, *Doctrines of Salvation*, comp. Bruce R. McConkie (1955), 2:90–91.
6. Lorenzo Snow in *Collected Discourses*, comp. Brian H. Stuy, 5 vols. (1987–92), 3:364.
7. Boyd K. Packer, "Our Moral Environment," *Ensign*, May 1992.

Fifteen

Always Retain a Remission of Your Sins

THE DAY I AM WRITING THIS CHAPTER IS THE DAY AFTER CHRISTMAS. We have spent the weekend in Bethlehem enjoying the Christmas commemorations and meeting with the members of our branch there. About a week ago, a couple in the branch had a new baby boy. We met him at church yesterday for the first time as our thoughts focused on baby Jesus born there many years ago.

Naturally, I have been thinking of Jesus our Savior and of His perfect and exemplary life. And sometimes, particularly as we are in deep sorrow or trial, our sinful lives seem so far distant from the perfect life of the Savior. The gulf seems so impassable. Yet the times of our deepest trial are likely the times we most desire an exalted life and perhaps the times we feel the most distant from such a life. But, in the eternal view, we are not as far removed as it seems now. Because of Jesus's birth in Bethlehem and His life, ministry, and Atonement, we may someday enjoy life like His. It was He, after all, who gave us the charge, "Be ye therefore perfect, even as your Father which is in heaven is perfect" (Matthew 5:48).

We reject the traditional teaching of *original sin* so prevalent in much of Christianity—that Adam and Eve sinned in their choice and role in the Fall and that, as a result, we as God's children are all born in sin and are "sinful" as we enter our mortality. We rather believe that we are blessed by the choice of Adam and Eve to be able to come to mortality and learn by our trials and experiences how to live the perfect life Heavenly Father desires to give us. We were *not born sinful*. We were rather born sin-free and innocent, but *we are born into a sinful world*. There is a big difference. The Lord declares, "Every spirit of man was innocent in the beginning; and God having redeemed man from the fall, men became again, in their infant state, innocent before God" (D&C 93:38).

Of course, we are all subject to the impositions of the Fall—we get sick, we have weeds in our gardens, we sorrow, we die, we divorce, and we are left to the temptations and buffetings of Satan wherein he tries to convince us that we are worthless, that we have failed, that we are sinful by nature, and that there is no hope for our redemption from such conditions. But just because we are subject to sin and the conditions of the Fall does not mean we are sinful by nature. We are godlike by our nature.

There is a big difference between the *Fall of Man* (the Fall of Adam and Eve) and the *Fall of Me*. *The Fall of Me* is the degree to which we individually choose things contrary to God's plan for us. We will all grow old and die because of the Fall, but we are free to choose whether or not we will sin. And of course, Jesus, the babe of Bethlehem, was the only person who ever maintained His sin-free innocence from birth to death—but that still does not mean we have to fall beyond salvation—we do not. In fact, the lesser the distance and depth of our personal fall—and we choose that distance—the happier we will be in this life and in the eternal world. We all sin, but we do not have to live out our lives enslaved to serious sin. We can be pure.

When we do sin, we "may speedily repent . . . and be restored to the blessings" (D&C 109:21) promised to us. If a person gets cancer, it is natural to seek treatment to put it into remission so he or she can live a pain-free and productive life. As we may develop the cancer of our soul through sin, it is certainly natural to desire remission of our sins—hopefully that desire remains to the end of our mortal lifetime so that we may continue toward eternal life.

Of the many teachings of and references to the concept of remission of our sins found throughout the scriptures, the fourth chapter of Mosiah has long been one of my favorites. This chapter comes after King Benjamin had already preached his classic sermon to his people about the grandeur of God and of His plan for us. Then, after observing the effect of his words upon the people, he once again spoke to them. I encourage my readers to explore the topic of remission of sins throughout the scriptures and to carefully conduct a complete reading and pondering of this particular chapter wherein King Benjamin charges his people, and us, that if we are humble and repentant, we will "always retain a remission of [our] sins" (Mosiah 4:12).

Mosiah taught the following principles to help his people retain a remission of their sins:

"Apply the atoning blood of Christ that we may receive forgiveness of our sins" (v. 2). We each sin, and we are each in need of repentance. If we wonder about what we need to do, our bishop can help us and bless us to know. In his role as appointed and authorized judge in Israel, he can also declare our worthiness, even when we sometimes do not see it for ourselves.

"Our hearts may be purified" (v. 2). We live in an impure world with temptation whispering—or shouting—at us from all directions. To have pure hearts, we need to learn how to tune out the world. It may mean limiting the media we view. It certainly means keeping our minds full of wholesomeness. This may appear as a daily grind throughout our lifetime, but we are capable of training our thoughts to a standard of purity. Living worthy of the Spirit and seeking it in all we do brings a sure promise of success.

"Having received a remission of their sins, and having peace of conscience" (v. 3). Consider the times of peace you have felt after reconciliation or repentance or after avoiding that which is evil. It is good and healthy to give ourselves occasional pause to always remember and seek after this peace of conscience.

"Be diligent in keeping his commandments" (v. 6). We know the commandments. It is for our good that we review them throughout our lives. Diligence in keeping the commandments is a daily task—but one that brings peace and joy.

"Continue in the faith even unto the end of his life" (v. 6). A man once told me that he "had promised the Lord that he would be obedient to the commandments for one year and see if he would be blessed." Although I commend any effort to live the gospel and although I was not a judge of this man—he would certainly be blessed for whatever effort he presented—I had the personal feeling that he had somewhat self-defeated before he began. We do not impose mortal time limits on an eternal being—the Lord's expectation is not for us to conduct a short-term trial run of obedience, but rather to make a lifelong commitment so that He may grant us eternal life, rather than a mere short-term trial run of joy.

"Believe that he has all wisdom, and all power, both in heaven and in earth" (v. 9). The more effort we make to know God, the better we will know Him. The more we serve others, the more we serve God. As we do so, we naturally come to know and to experience His power in all the world and in our personal lives.

"Believe that ye must repent of your sins and forsake them" (v. 10). I am writing this chapter with the assumption that all of us who are reading it agree that we need constant repentance. "If we say that we have no sin, we deceive ourselves, and the truth is not in us" (1 John 1:8).

"Ask in sincerity of heart that he would forgive you" (v. 10). Having faith in Jesus Christ is having faith that He really does have the power to forgive sins. His power to forgive is not restrained nor increased by the degree of our faith—He works at constant full capacity to forgive. "He is mighty to save" (Alma 34:18). We self-impose limits because of our own insincerity and less-than-perfect faith—we do well to work to diligently increase our faith.

"Always retain in remembrance the greatness of God" (v. 11). There are many ways to retain the greatness of God in our remembrance. Worshipping in the temple, serving others, praying in humility, pondering the night sky, counting our many blessings, and sharing our testimonies of truth with others are all good ways.

"[Stand] steadfastly in the faith of that which is to come" (v. 11). As I currently live in East Jerusalem and travel regularly through the separation wall into the West Bank for our service in the Bethlehem Branch, I see daily evidence of the deep-rooted conflicts of this land. The more I observe, the more convinced I become that the Second Coming of Christ will provide the only lasting and complete solution. Personally, I stand steadfastly in my faith that He really will come and finally bring peace to these beautiful souls. And although I know that our hearts can be healed here in our mortality, I believe that the Lord has marvelous future blessings in store in the next world for those who are willing to accept Him and stand fast in our testimonies of Him.

"Ye shall always rejoice, and be filled with the love of God, and always retain a remission of your sins" (v. 12). Through our sincere repentance, we can hasten the day of forgiveness of our sins. Once forgiven, if we are sincere, we will desire to always keep our sins in remission. Along with our rejection of the sectarian notion of original sin, we also reject the concept of eternal damnation, implying everlasting burning of unrepentant souls in a huge lake of fire and brimstone. "Eternal punishment" and "Endless punishment" are not so named because they have no end—they are so named because they constitute God's system of punishment and are named after Him—"Eternal" and "Endless" are His names:

> For, behold, the mystery of godliness, how great is it! For, behold, I am endless, and the punishment which is given from my hand is endless punishment, for Endless is my name. Wherefore—
> Eternal punishment is God's punishment.
> Endless punishment is God's punishment. (D&C 19:10–12)

Our suffering need only last long enough to achieve our repentance—and then we may keep our sins in remission so we need not suffer again.

"Not have a mind to injure one another, but to live peaceably" (v. 13). This counsel has obvious application to our dealings with all of humanity. But such an attitude of not causing injury to one another is particularly needful and essential among all of the players in our divorce. Our life and the lives of our children will be greatly blessed as we cause no harm of any kind to our former spouse. The more we can live in peace with others, the more we will be at peace with ourselves.

"Not suffer your children that they go hungry . . . transgress . . . quarrel" (v. 14). It is challenging enough to teach and help our children under non-stressful times in life. The challenges are accentuated during divorce, but teaching children to do right is still needful. In speaking of times of trial and strain in families, the First Presidency has declared, "Disability, death, or other circumstances may necessitate individual adaptation. Extended families should lend support when needed."[1] Divorce is a family affair—and the family may need to extend to include teachers, scout leaders, and other good people to be part of the team for teaching and helping our children.

"I give not because I have not, but if I had I would give" (v. 24). We are generally more capable at some times than at other times in life to give and help those in need. As my wife and I are engaged in humanitarian service here in Jerusalem, we have learned that there is and always will be more of a need than we have resources to fill. But we do what we can and try to decline our help gracefully when we must. We have also concluded that when Satan is finally put in check and the resources of the earth no longer go toward war and oppression, there will be more than enough to provide for all of Heavenly Father's children with plenty to spare—just as He said (see D&C 104:15–17).

"In wisdom and order; for it is not requisite that a man should run faster than he has strength" (v. 27). After my divorce, there were times that I perhaps tried to push the timetable too hard in order to fix all that had gone wrong. If I had to do it over again, I could have been wiser—but time has moved on and I am where I now am. But we can only do so much so fast. I think we need to seek the Spirit and counsel with those we trust to help us know what to do and when to do it. The Lord is patient with us, even when we may not be with ourselves.

"Watch yourselves . . . thoughts . . . words . . . deeds" (v. 30). Self-control is always fashionable with the Lord, and it needs to be so particularly during divorce or other stressful times of life. Part of our fallen nature is that we are subject to the lusts and temptations of the flesh. And although the choice is ours how we react to such, if we desire healing and remission of our sins, we must learn to keep ourselves in check. Even though King Solomon struggled to apply his own wisdom, he did give wise counsel, "For as he thinketh in his heart, so is he" (Proverbs 23:7).

My home community has a reputation for clever bumper stickers. A few years ago, I saw one that read, "If you think education is expensive, try ignorance." Prompted by this thought-provoking saying, I have coined a few of my own, such as, "If you think worthiness a burden, try sin." The suffering for serious sin should remind anyone of the better course of not sinning to begin with, or truly repenting when we have sinned.

As we come to know the peace and joy of repentance of our sins, we will be naturally motivated to keep our sins in remission—to live continually free of the burden of sin. As we do our part of accepting the gospel of Jesus Christ, repenting of our sins, and aligning our lives with the path to eternal life, the Holy Ghost will fulfill His divine mission of cleansing us of sin, "And after they had been received unto baptism, and were wrought upon and cleansed by the power of the Holy Ghost, they were numbered among the people of the church of Christ; and their names were taken, that they might be remembered and nourished by the good word of God, to keep them in the right way, to keep them continually watchful unto prayer, relying alone upon the merits of Christ, who was the author and the finisher of their faith" (Moroni 6:4).

Nephi taught, "Wherefore, do the things which I have told you I have seen that your Lord and your Redeemer should do; for, for this cause have they been shown unto me, that ye might know the gate by which ye should enter. For the gate by which ye should enter is repentance and baptism by water; and then cometh a remission of your sins by fire and by the Holy Ghost" (2 Nephi 31:17).

Repenting of our sins can be challenging work, but it is sweet work and much more ennobling than the alternative. As we accomplish our repentance, we receive the peace and joy of having made eternal, positive investments in our own soul and in the souls of those we love.

Note

1. "The Family: A Proclamation to the World," *Ensign* or *Liahona*, Nov. 2010, 129.

Sixteen

True Enduring

DURING ONE OF THE DARKEST HOURS OF MY TRIAL OF DIVORCE, I experienced what I have felt was a godsend or a small miracle or a tender mercy or whatever we may be wont to call it. (I believe that things do not have to seem miraculous to be miracles. I appreciate God's help no matter how small and insignificant the method may seem.) I was at my assignment at the Church Office Building and felt the need to be alone. During my lunch break, I sought out an empty room and entered to ponder and pray. As I entered, I was intrigued by a statement that had been written on the whiteboard, without a reference, which had been partially erased. I was inspired enough by what I could discern from the statement that I researched the source and found the complete statement. It has become another guiding star of my life and I hope it will be of value to you. Here is the quotation from Elder Neal A. Maxwell:

> Therefore, true enduring represents not merely the passage of time, but the passage of the soul—and not merely from A to B, but sometimes all the way from A to Z. To endure in faith and doeth God's will (see D&C 63:20; D&C 101:35) therefore involves much more than putting up with a circumstance.
>
> Rather than shoulder-shrugging, true enduring is soul-trembling. Jesus bled not at a few, but "at every pore" (D&C 19:18).
>
> Sometimes spiritual obedience requires us to "hold on" lovingly, such as to a rebellious child, while others cry, "Let go!" Enduring may likewise mean, however, "letting go," when everything within us wants to "hold on," such as to a loved one "appointed unto death" (D&C 42:48).
>
> Patient endurance permits us to cling to our faith in the Lord and our faith in His timing when we are being tossed about by the surf of circumstance. Even when a seeming undertow grasps us, somehow, in the tumbling, we are being carried forward, though battered and

bruised.... When, for the moment, we ourselves are not being stretched on a particular cross, we ought to be at the foot of someone else's—full of empathy and proffering spiritual refreshment.[1]

The simple, sublime power of this quote for me is that it declares our healing process, *the passage of the soul*, and then declares our mission to turn our energies to the well-being of others—*full of empathy and proffering spiritual refreshment.*

THE PASSAGE OF THE SOUL

As Elder Maxwell taught, mere passage of time does not equate with the spiritual growth of our souls. If we are doing nothing more than waiting for time to pass and hoping this trial will soon end, we will likely be disappointed with the end result. I have often been guilty of this "I just want this to end" attitude, and it has not been for my good.

True endurance involves soul growth. People do not automatically experience the same growth from similar trying circumstances. In my teaching of a particular principle about war in the Book of Mormon, I have sometimes shared the contrasted soul growth of two Vietnam veterans—one a dear friend and the other a mere acquaintance. They both experienced the front-line horrors of the war.

My friend came home mellowed and softened by his experience. He was my fellow teacher, and we formed an instant bond of friendship. I requested that he serve as my counselor at the Missionary Training Center, and I marveled and delighted in the sweet, gentle way he taught and counseled our missionaries. He was full of the Spirit and full of love for the sisters and elders; his very presence blessed their lives. His teachings grounded them in true doctrine and prepared them for their mission and life service. His war service was not a wasted year—it was a year of exponential growth of his soul.

The second man was one of my commanders from my time in military basic training. I have since wondered what became of him. At the time of my association with him, he was between tours of duty and was a bitter and hateful man with a perpetual scowl and a terrible temper. We learned to avoid him as much as possible. Some of my buddies convinced me to go to a war movie one weekend at the Post theatre and we coincidentally sat several rows behind this man. That is my only recollection of seeing him laugh—as people were slaughtered in the battles.

The Book of Mormon records, "But behold, because of the exceedingly great length of the war between the Nephites and the Lamanites *many had become hardened*, because of the exceedingly great length of the war; and *many were softened* because of their afflictions, insomuch that they did humble themselves before God, even in the depth of humility" (Alma 62:41; emphasis added).

Of course we acknowledge that in God's infinite love and judgment, He will suit "his mercies according to the conditions of the children of men" (D&C 46:15). But there seems to be ample opportunity for free choice of how we will react to our trials—we can certainly choose to follow Satan or to follow Christ. And granted, sometimes in war, lines are blurred and good people must do terrible things, but God knows hearts and will bless and sustain the sincere efforts of those who choose to be humble and seek to serve God. This principle also holds true in divorce—we may not choose for another and their choices may hurt us, but we do get to choose how we react to the hurt. And as we choose the good part, God will remain faithful to us with His hand stretched out to help us along.

One of my favorite images from my study and writing of the prophet Isaiah is his description of God's mercy, love, and desire to rescue and save His children. Even as we suffer from poor choices and feel the chastisement of God, He stands with "his hand . . . stretched out still" (Isaiah 10:4) to lead and help us along. Elder George Q. Cannon taught:

> No matter how serious the trial, how deep the distress, how great the affliction, [God] will never desert us. He never has, and He never will. He cannot do it. It is not His character [to do so]. . . . He will [always] stand by us. We may pass through the fiery furnace; we may pass through deep waters; but we shall not be consumed nor overwhelmed. We shall emerge from all these trials and difficulties the better and purer for them.[2]

Of course, I would not have chosen divorce. I could have learned and progressed from other trials, and would have much preferred such. But it did happen and I—like all of us—am left with my agency paired to my trials. My sister counseled me to be patient and alert to the life lessons the Lord would teach me through the trial. It seemed impossible then, but now I see it. I have learned much, and so can you.

Although perhaps a painful task, I invite you to join me in some serious post-divorce life questioning:

- Do I better understand the doctrine of humility?
- Am I less judgmental of other people—particularly of those divorced?
- Do I better recognize my dependence upon God?
- Do I remember the feelings I have had during the process of divorce?
- Have these feelings increased my empathy for others?
- Do I have a clearer understanding of and feeling for the infinite Atonement of our Savior?
- Do I feel more love for humanity?
- Is repentance more personal in my life than before?
- Am I more patient with others when they make mistakes?
- Do I better understand and feel the doctrine of forgiveness?
- Do I read scriptures with new understanding of how they apply to my life?
- Do I feel greater compassion for the suffering souls of all the world?
- Am I more grateful for the goodness of God to me and to my family?

After considering these questions, if your conclusions are not positive and do not demonstrate increased growth and faith, I invite you to patiently plod forward in seeking reconciliation and peace through your trials. And I remind you that as you do so, the Lord's hand is stretched out to you to help you and guide you.

If your conclusions to my sample questions (and many more such questions left unasked) are positive, then I believe that you are undergoing what Elder Maxwell calls "true enduring" and that you are experiencing a true and productive passage of the soul. You are not just marking time—you are marching forward and are more fully preparing to engage in "proffering spiritual refreshment" to others.

FULL OF EMPATHY AND PROFFERING SPIRITUAL REFRESHMENT

King Benjamin asked, "For behold, are we not all beggars? Do we not all depend upon the same Being, even God, for all the substance which we have, for both food and raiment, and for gold, and for silver, and for all the riches which we have of every kind?" (Mosiah 4:19). Of course, we are all beggars. And we "all are alike unto God" (2 Nephi 26:33).

Now I invite you to conduct another brief exercise. Go back and consider the questions I asked of us in the previous section and make them real and specific in your life. For example, who do you know who has divorced, and how has your perception of and empathy for this person changed because of your own divorce? Take some time and try to identify your specific thoughts and feelings. Do you love them more? Are you less willing to pass judgment and more willing to listen to and serve them because of your divorce? See, you are experiencing the true passage of your soul (assuming positive answers). This is a great blessing stemming from your divorce and your positive choice of how you are dealing with it. Now I invite you to continue this soul-growth analysis with other questions of your own making. I think you will find that your soul is growing greater than perhaps you have given yourselves credit for and that your mercy for self and others is increasing.

The Prophet Joseph Smith taught a sweet doctrine about mercy and soul growth: "The nearer we get to our heavenly Father, the more we are disposed to look with compassion on perishing souls; we feel that we want to take them upon our shoulders, and cast their sins behind our backs. My talk is intended for all this society; if you would have God have mercy on you, have mercy on one another."[3]

My wife and I have been prompted toward "proffering spiritual refreshment" to others in regard to healing from our divorces. I believe Heavenly Father is encouraging others through the experience of our trials.

For example, at the time of my assignment as the Institute director in Wisconsin, I was counseled to be wise about over-sharing the experiences of my divorce—and I understood. The goal of all official Church curriculum courses and gospel instructors is to teach success in marriage. But one day in a very small class, I was prompted to share my story and experiences. One young lady was absent that day but was told of the discussion by her husband, who had attended. When I saw her again, she excitedly asked if they could perhaps come over for dinner sometime and discuss more of the matter. Of course they could.

We enjoyed a beautiful fall day with this young couple hiking and lunching. The young lady told us the story of her own healing process in regard to her childhood broken family. She was valiantly strong and had led her younger siblings in escape of a dangerous home environment by running away in the nighttime to the safety of extended family. She expressed her love and gratitude to us for being willing to share our experiences and for trying to now live the best we could as examples of healing and soul-growth.

We've also been given opportunity at the BYU Jerusalem Center for Near Eastern Studies. Here we serve as a hosting and humanitarian service couple, and not in any type of a formal teaching role. However, apparently I have attracted a bit of attention by my writing of this book because I have peculiarly perched myself before my computer during my off-duty hours in various spots at the center and on trips. Various students have stopped to chat and have even inquired as to what I am doing. This has prompted several conversations with some whose parents or siblings have divorced.

We have seen light and hope in their eyes as my wife and I have shared with them how we took a daring plunge into our second marriage on the premise that we trusted one another to be steadfast and immovable in keeping our gospel covenants. They have confided to us their fears about marriage. They have come back to us and thanked us for the counsel and example given them. We are happy that we have been able to, in some small way, proffer love, empathy, and encouragement to these wonderful souls who only seek true happiness in life. Heavenly Father did not cause our trial but has now orchestrated it to the blessing and encouragement of others—and for that we are grateful.

As you struggle through the dark, sorrowful hours of your trial, hang on tightly to your faith. Diligently endure. Allow the Lord to help you discover who you really are—and I believe you will like the discovery. Morning light will follow your night of darkness and with it will come blessings and comfort and healing that you could never before imagine.

Notes

1. Neal A. Maxwell, "'Endure It Well,'" *Ensign*, May 1990.
2. George Q. Cannon, "Remarks," *Deseret Evening News*, Mar. 7, 1891, 4.
3. Joseph Smith Jr., *Teachings of the Prophet Joseph Smith*, comp. Joseph Fielding Smith (Salt Lake City: Deseret Book, 1976), 241.

Seventeen

Trust in the Lord, and in Thyself

"Faith is not to have a perfect knowledge of things; therefore if ye have faith ye hope for things which are not seen, which are true" (Alma 32:21). Even though my own marriage had failed, I knew that marriage was a true and eternal principle. I had always wanted a true marriage—and hoped for one, although after my divorce I could not see how it would happen or where it would take me. But even though my heart was broken, I was intent on healing and moving forward.

I trust my sister—she has always been true and faithful. She invited me to her home in Chicago as a respite to sort things out. While there, somewhat at my urging, she called Carol, a longtime friend of hers, who had divorced and moved back to her home in Wisconsin. I had wanted to go to the temple, and when we learned that Carol was going on Saturday, we went then. Meeting someone in the temple is not foolproof but certainly increases trust and confidence and helps to answer many of the normal questions one might have about such things as commitment and worthiness.

Carol and I met, exchanged contact information, and began a correspondence. She visited Utah and I visited Wisconsin. Within a few months, we were sealed together in the Chicago temple. I trusted her faith and her testimony. I trusted her courage to marry someone so down and out as I was. And deep down, although shaken to my core by the breakup of my family and the loss of my profession, I trusted myself. I knew I could work hard and could continue in keeping my covenants, and I hoped that I could find meaningful employment—preferably by a return to my beloved profession.

Seventeen: *Trust in the Lord, and in Thyself*

Steadfast and *immovable* were the trigger words that prompted our plunge into our marriage. Once we discovered our common desire and commitment to be such, we married. We have always tried to trust the Lord throughout our marriage, through its many joys but through its challenges as well, starting with the blending of families and the reconciliation of strong wills. Through our married years, we have generally cared for others in our home, including my aged mother, my wife's aged aunt, and, at times, struggling children and grandchildren. We have had our heartaches with the wandering and even death of loved ones. And then just over a year ago, we realized that our home had become an empty nest, so we began an inquiry that brought us to Jerusalem. Where we go next in life is yet to be determined, but we are confident that we will go forth in love as we try to be steadfast and immovable in keeping our covenants. We trust that the Lord will continue to guide us and lead us along into opportunities to grow and to be of service in His kingdom and to His children.

Through experience, study, and faith, I have discovered that the foundation to healing from divorce is to trust the Lord in all things. And as we do, we will be inspired and guided to trust in ourselves and to know and seek out others we can trust.

The profundity of one of my lifelong favorite scriptural passages has been accentuated by the experiences of my divorce.

> Trust in the Lord with all thine heart; and lean not unto thine own understanding.
>
> In all thy ways acknowledge him, and he shall direct thy paths. (Proverbs 3:5–6)

I have come to know that, although many in our world are untrustworthy, our Savior is always trustworthy:

> Thus saith the Lord, Where is the bill of your mother's divorcement, whom I have put away? or which of my creditors is it to whom I have sold you? Behold, for your iniquities have ye sold yourselves, and for your transgressions is your mother put away. (Isaiah 50:1)

The implication is, of course, that there is no bill of divorcement—the Lord will never abandon nor forsake us, even though we sometimes forsake Him and each other. The Lord then reminds us of His grandeur and power to save:

> Is my hand shortened at all, that it cannot redeem? or have I no power to deliver? behold, at my rebuke I dry up the sea, I make the rivers a wilderness: their fish stinketh, because there is no water, and dieth for thirst.
>
> I clothe the heavens with blackness, and I make sackcloth their covering.
>
> The Lord God hath given me the tongue of the learned, that I should know how to speak a word in season to him that is weary: he wakeneth morning by morning, he wakeneth mine ear to hear as the learned. (vs. 2–4)

The Lord, who has the power to move heaven and earth, has the power to redeem us and to heal our broken hearts.

As we now approach the conclusion of this book, let us revisit Emily Hill Woodmansee's life as an example to us of one who trusted the Lord—and herself. Emily, as is true of each of us, continued to have many trials throughout her lifetime in addition to the trials of her divorce. The successful passing of one test does not exempt us from further tutoring by the Lord.

In Emily's case, after her husband betrayed her, she was left in dire economic circumstances. At one point, the house in which she was living was sold. As she contemplated the frightening prospect of being homeless, one night she received a powerful spiritual inspiration to pen her thoughts into words. She states:

> One night when I was so weary with overwork and anxiety, pondering what to do, these words impressed me as if audibly spoken, 'Trust in God and thyself.' Instantly I arose and composed the following lines:

> A precious boon! is a friend indeed,
> Greet him as such when his face you see;
> But those who fail thee in time of need—
> Shun them as false friends should shunned be.
> They proffer this, and they promise that,
> But promise, also, is a doubtful elf.
> So would'st thou weather the storm of life—
> Trust thou in God! and thyself.
>
> Keep a brave heart, though the waves roll high!
> Let thine aim be true as the magnet's steel;
> Look unto God! with a steadfast eye,

Seventeen: *Trust in the Lord, and in Thyself*

And trust him always, in woe or weal,
Man may deceive, but God is true;
Mortals may pander to lover or pelf,
Like "angel's visits" firm friends are few,
Trust thou in God! and thyself.

Should friends, nor fortune, nor home be thine—
Cringe not for this, nor beg for that;
The earnest seekers will surely find
Something to thoroughly labor at.
'Tis a cheering maxim to keep in view—
That diligence leads to plenty's shelf;
And whatsoever thy hands pursue—
Trust thou in God! and thyself.

What though thy flesh and thy strength should fail?
Surely 'twere better to wear than rust;
Than never to try, t'were better to die,
In striving bravely to fill our trust;
But fear not thou, for God is good—
He is the giver of strength and wealth.
When faithless feelings or friends intrude—
Trust thou in God! and thyself.[1]

Emily did not quit. She put one foot in front of the other and kept her face toward Zion as she battled the storms of life.[2] She was also humble enough to accept help from a trusted friend, President Heber J. Grant, who shared this experience of Emily's courage and indomitable will:

> While sitting in the bank one day the Spirit whispered to me that Sister Emily H. Woodmansee was in financial need. I accordingly drew from my account at the bank $50 and proceeded with it to her home. On the way I debated whether I should present this to her as a gift, or offer it to her as a loan. Fearing I might offend her, as I remembered her high spirit, I decided upon the latter course. As I shook hands with her I offered her the money as a loan, without interest, with promise never to accept it until she was in comfortable enough circumstance to return it of her own choice.
>
> With tears in her eyes Sister Emily confessed that she and her family were almost destitute. Twenty-five dollars of it was immediately spent for provisions and coal. With the remaining twenty-five dollars she took an option on a piece of property. In thirty days she sold the

property for $700. With this she bought and sold many other parcels of real estate, showing the keenest sagacity and wisdom in the business world. It is needless to say the $50 was returned with thanks to me, and praises to God, for a true friend in her hour of need.[3]

After my remarriage and during my continuing struggles to regain my profession and meet the challenges of helping our children, my bishop and I had a simple and sweet connecting experience. I was his home teacher and personal friend. We talked often of life and its trials and purposes. He was struggling with a major life decision concerning his employment. As we discovered after the fact, we both received a simultaneous powerful witness of the goodness of the Lord and of His commitment to guide our lives. In our sacrament meeting that day, through one of our hymns we were both inspired, edified, and encouraged to keep pressing forward in faith:

> Where can I turn for peace?
> Where is my solace
> When other sources cease to make me whole?
> When with a wounded heart, anger, or malice,
> I draw myself apart,
> Searching my soul?
>
> Where, when my aching grows,
> Where, when I languish,
> Where, in my need to know, where can I run?
> Where is the quiet hand to calm my anguish?
> Who, who can understand?
> He, only One.
>
> He answers privately,
> Reaches my reaching
> In my Gethsemane, Savior and Friend.
> Gentle the peace he finds for my beseeching.
> Constant he is and kind,
> Love without end.[4]

When it seems that we cannot trust others or perhaps even ourselves, we can always trust the Lord. And through His kind and constant tutoring, He prepares us to be self-reliant and to trust in our own abilities, our past revelations and successes, and our future potential.

When Oliver Cowdery struggled with desire for further guidance and wisdom in the midst of new challenges and opportunities, the Lord inspired him by having him look back to the foundations of his faith, "Did I not speak peace to your mind concerning this matter? What greater witness can you have than from God?" (D&C 6:23). The beauty of trusting the Lord is that when He speaks truth to us, we can count on His wisdom and instruction to always be true and constant. He will never divorce us.

Notes

1. Edith Ivins Lamoreaux, "Sweet Singers of Zion: Life Sketches of Emily Hill Woodmansee and Julia Hill Ivins," *Relief Society Magazine* 8, no. 10 (1921): 565–566.
2. Emily H. Woodmansee also wrote the words to a hymn in our modern hymnal, *As Sisters in Zion* (*Hymns*, no. 309). Through the words of this hymn, Emily continues to inspire others by her faith and courage.
3. Edith Ivins Lamoreaux, "Sweet Singers of Zion: Life Sketches of Emily Hill Woodmansee and Julia Hill Ivins," *Relief Society Magazine* 8, no. 10 (1921): 566–567.
4. "Where Can I Turn for Peace," *Hymns of the Church of Jesus Christ of Latter-day Saints*, no. 129.

Epilogue

The Piercing Light of the Savior's Atonement

NEAR THE BEGINNING OF THIS WRITING, WE CITED ELDER BRUCE C. Hafen, wherein he taught that the Atonement of Jesus Christ can compensate for all of our shortcomings and failures. Let us draw from his wisdom once again to glimpse the outcome of demonstrating faith through struggles:

> Whether we descend into the dark night of our own soul through transgression, unwise choices, natural opposition, the invitation of God, or some mixture of causes, the crucial issue is whether we can in that experience yield our broken hearts contritely to God. This willingness to sacrifice all things must reach broadly and deeply enough to include the sacrifice of our sins, our vanity, our self-esteem, and our love of worldly comforts. Sometimes we must also sacrifice our determination to understand to our rational satisfaction why we should be lost in the darkness. When the light of the Savior's atoning power finally pierces that darkness, compensating for our bitterness and carrying us up the cycle to reconciliation and re-unity with God, the blessing of understanding will finally be ours, one result of "arriving where we started and knowing the place for the first time."[1]

Through my experience, my study, and the exercise of my faith, I have come to believe that the Atonement enables us to arise from the ashes of life and come into the full glory and fellowship of our Heavenly Father in His kingdom. In the meantime, life is hard and scary. We will have disappointments and heartaches seemingly more than we can bear at times. I have often felt that way. But the fact that I am still here and still trying to move my life forward is testimony of the goodness of the Lord to me and my family. I have mostly given up on trying to figure out the "why" of all of my life trials. I trust that I will understand in due time. Instead, I am trying to focus on the "why" of the Lord's great plan of happiness for all people—and specifically for me and mine. It is that He loves us and desires to give us all that He can possible give. I trust Him. I believe Him. I love Him.

I share this quote from President Howard W. Hunter that I have likely quoted more than any other in my gospel teaching, "Please remember this one thing. If our lives and our faith are centered upon Jesus Christ and his restored gospel, nothing can ever go permanently wrong. On the other hand, if our lives are not centered on the Savior and his teachings, no other success can ever be permanently right."[2]

"Permanently" seems to be a key word here. Yes, divorce all seems so wrong—especially as we are in the depths of it. But the effects need not be *permanent*. I trust that each of you—whatever your specific trials have been or will be—will be able to find *permanent* peace to your souls and healing to your broken hearts and that we may all be "made perfect through Jesus the mediator of the new covenant, who wrought out this perfect atonement through the shedding of his own blood" (D&C 76:69).

Bless You,

Reg Christensen
Waunakee, Wisconsin

Notes

1. Bruce C. Hafen, *The Broken Heart: Applying the Atonement to Life's Experiences* (Salt Lake City: Deseret Book, 2008), 64–65.
2. Howard W. Hunter, "Fear Not, Little Flock," *1988–89 Devotional and Fireside Speeches* (Provo: Brigham Young University Press, 1989), 112. https://speeches.byu.edu/talks/howard-w-hunter_fear-little-flock.

Acknowledgments

Thank you to my family and many friends who have encouraged this project, reviewed the manuscript, and offered such valuable counsel and correction.

Thank you to my professional editor and publisher who always do such a great job.

Thank you to all of you everywhere who reach out with a hand of healing to those who suffer. Your caring compassion will be eternally remembered and rewarded.

About the Author

Reg Christensen and his wife, Carol, live in Waunakee, Wisconsin. They are the parents of seven and grandparents of sixteen. Reg is a teacher and author. The goal and theme of his teaching and writing is *Liken unto Us*—relating and applying the principles of the gospel to our personal lives by trusting in the Lord and His Atonement. Reg retired in Wisconsin as the Church Educational System coordinator for the Green Bay, Madison, and Wausau stakes and as director of the Institute of Religion adjacent to the University of Wisconsin in Madison. He began his CES career in Lehi, Utah, where he taught released-time seminary for twenty-three years. Reg has enjoyed a lifetime of Church service as a missionary, Young Men's president, bishopric counselor, high councilor, stake executive secretary, branch president, bishop, high priest group leader, ward clerk, district clerk, and ward seminary teacher. He and Carol recently served as missionaries for the Brigham Young University–Idaho Pathway program and, at the time of this writing, are living in East Jerusalem on an eighteen-month

About the Author

term of volunteer service at the Brigham Young University Jerusalem Center for Near Eastern Studies. Their responsibilities are tour hosting and humanitarian outreach. Their current Church callings are in the Bethlehem branch with Carol as Relief Society president and Reg as branch president. Reg is a tradesman and handyman and enjoys reading, writing, woodworking, leathercraft, travel, exploring nature, bird watching, and being with family and friends.

Scan to visit

www.regchristensen.com